If good governance is a habit—which Ted Hull asserts strongly that it is—then this book will help your church move toward habitually governing well. With wit and wisdom, Ted draws from his rich and practical experience in church life and organizational governance to assist churches in understanding and applying Policy Governance® consistently and correctly.

Knowing Ted personally affirms my trust in him as a man who loves the church, understands the church, and wants God's best for the church. Knowing Ted professionally affirms my trust in him as an expert in the field of Policy Governance, with keen insights into why and how boards should best govern. In short, this book brings an effective model of governance, tested and refined in real life environments, to the church.

As I worked through each chapter of this book, I was struck by how each section just makes sense when thinking about the reasons for and the practices of Policy Governance. When put together, the sequence of thought regarding board development is logical and comprehensive. The questions Ted Hull asks about church boards are insightful; the answers are clear and razor sharp. By the end of this work, you'll wonder how your board has survived without these intense understandings and instructive practical concepts. Reading this book might not save your church unnecessary board governance confusion and conflict, but reading and applying it as a habit very well might. I highly recommend Ted Hull's newest book to you and your church board.

Daniel Hamil, Ed.D.
Executive Director/CEO
North American Baptist Conference

In *Focusing Your Church Board*, Ted Hull speaks to all those involved in trying to bring Christian faith into people's lives through the operation of a church. As we all know, the very best intentions can go astray unless focused on a productive path. This book is intended to encourage church board members and pastors to consider a more effective and focused approach to governance.

In amusing and easily accessible style, Ted offers hope that there is a way to make a meaningful difference at the board level. This is not so much a "how to" book (a subject covered by other resources in this book's bibliography) but more a source of rationale and inspiration for embarking on a new governance journey at all. All brought to life by tales from Ted's extensive experience at the sharp end of good intentions.

Caroline Oliver, CEO
International Policy Governance Association

When typical ministry situations tempt our church leaders to follow the loudest voice or favorite program, it is good to have a book that helps with *Focusing Your Church Board*. I know of no better governance system to offer boards than John Carver's Policy Governance®. And Ted is to be commended for providing this resource in a practical and understandable way. Those with the courage and discipline to use this powerful tool are likely to find themselves and their church moving to a new level of mission accomplishment for the glory of God.

Dr. Phil Graybeal, governance consultant
Graybeal and Associates, LLC
Greer, SC

Reflect on the last few church board meetings you attended. Did the board spend more time talking about the church's purpose—the difference your local congregation should make in people's lives, in the community and in the world beyond—or talking about maintaining the building, the type of music used, how to increase attendance, and how to raise more funds? Ted Hull approaches the topic of church governance in an engaging style that has you laughing and nodding one moment, and shaking your head in dismay the next as he describes governance practices that are all too common, but focused on maintenance instead of mission. He clearly outlines how applying a complete system of governance (Policy Governance®) can help a church board function as effectively as possible in focusing attention on mission. I have worked with this system for over 20 years and can attest to its value. Because applying it well can dramatically increase the effectiveness of church board leadership, it is my prayer that church boards seriously consider its potential. Even if you tend to be a "doubting Thomas," I urge you to suspend your doubts long enough to read and absorb the message of this book.

Jannice Moore
President, The Governance Coach™

When it comes to leadership and governance in the church, getting it right is imperative. Anything less means misdirected energy and wasted resources. Policy Governance® is a powerful and empowering foundation for getting it right. Good governance doesn't just happen. Consistent practise is not optional. In the words of coaching legend, Vince Lombardi, "Practise does not make perfect, only perfect practise makes perfect". Knowing that while we will never be perfect, we can improve as we strive to practise governance and leadership with a view to excellence. Ted's latest book is a great resource that you will be reaching for as you seek to align your practices with this biblically consistent and logically sequential governance system. Ted uses pointed questions and practical illustrations to reinforce an understanding of the principles and practise of Policy Governance. Each chapter offers clear insight to help boards and leaders identify successes, opportunities for improvement, and systematic practices for accountability. Common pitfalls are identified so your board can assess if it has ventured into faulty practises or vague expectations. If your church or organization is initiating Policy Governance or if you are seasoned veterans in the governance arena, *Focusing Your Church Board* will be invaluable in getting leadership right and establishing accountability for success.

Ken Wilson, Executive Pastor
Grant Memorial Church, Winnipeg, MB

Focusing Your
CHURCH
BOARD

USING THE CARVER POLICY
GOVERNANCE MODEL

TED HULL

FOCUSING YOUR CHURCH BOARD
Copyright © 2015 by Ted Hull

All rights reserved. Neither this publication nor any part of this publication may be reproduced or transmitted in any form or by any means, electronic or mechanical, including photocopying, recording or any information storage and retrieval system, without permission in writing from the author.

Policy Governance® is an internationally registered service mark of John Carver. Registration is only to ensure accurate description of the model rather than for financial gain. The model is available free to all with no royalties or license fees for its use. The authoritative website for Policy Governance is www. carvergovernance.com

Scripture quotations are from the ESV® Bible (The Holy Bible, English Standard Version®), copyright © 2001 by Crossway, a publishing ministry of Good News Publishers. Used by permission. All rights reserved.

ISBN: 978-1-4866-0897-3

Word Alive Press
131 Cordite Road, Winnipeg, MB R3W 1S1
www.wordalivepress.ca

WORD ALIVE
—P R E S S—

Library and Archives Canada Cataloguing in Publication
Hull, Ted, 1951-, author
    Focusing your church board: using the Carver policy governance model / Ted Hull.
Issued in print and electronic formats.
ISBN 978-1-4866-0897-3 (pbk.).--ISBN 978-1-4866-0898-0 (pdf).--
ISBN 978-1-4866-0899-7 (html).--ISBN 978-1-4866-0900-0 (epub)

    1. Church committees. 2. Church management. 3. Christian leadership. I. Title.
BV652.H84 2015   262'.22   C2015-902533-8
                                        C2015-902534-6

Policy Governance is not capitalized in the above Library and Archives Canada Cataloguing in Publication record in consistency with their directives.

Acknowledgements

L iterally hundreds of people have had input into this book. They include staff I have served with as well as board members who have shared their expertise, experiences, and frustrations. It's the cumulative effects of your input for which I am thankful.

Bill Ehlers, you first introduced me to Policy Governance. Little did you (or I) know what the ongoing impact of that conversation would be.

Miriam Carver, who packed years of experience and hundreds of stories into the Policy Governance® Academy^SM, of which I was privileged to be a part. Thank you for letting me in, even if at times you must have questioned your wisdom.

Caroline Oliver, who reviewed the book for consistency with the Policy Governance model. The readers have benefited more than they know from your ninety-nine comments (no, not one hundred) and the hundreds of corrections you graciously contributed to the accuracy and readability of this book.

Eric Craymer, Phil Graybeal, Barry Packer, and Richard Stringham, whose comments kindly pushed me to sharpen both my thinking and my writing. Thank you for your time and expertise.

Jannice Moore, thank you for reading my book on a flight from Chicago to Calgary and then so graciously and generously affirming it.

Evan Braun, thank you for the way you professionally and patiently edited what you had to work with. You made me look better.

Jen Jandavs-Hedlin and Amy Groening at Word Alive Press, your kindness and patience with me is overwhelming. I suggested the perfect title, and then I didn't want it. My indecision and nebulous complaints must have nearly plumbed the depths of your patience, but you never complained. You provided invaluable input and influence, including the color scheme. (I so badly wanted purple.)

Lorna, I am grateful and appreciative of your patience toward me when I disappeared to rewrite and re-edit. I love you.

Thank You, Heavenly Father, for breathing into me a passion for being part of nudging Your Kingdom forward in this way. It could only come from You.

INTRODUCTION

My book had recently been awarded the Christian Leadership book of the year by The Word Guild when I met a friend for lunch. With delight, he embraced one of his callings in life—embarrassing me. He introduced me to the server by pointing out that I was an award-winning author.

"Oh," she responded with the appropriate amount of enthusiasm. "What kind of book is it?"

I gave my friend a "nice going, buddy" look and mumbled the title: *A Guide to Governing Charities.*

"Congratulations," she replied flatly. "Are you gentlemen ready to order yet?"

Even an award-winning book about governance doesn't cultivate much enthusiasm from the most ardent reader, and a casual conversation about the subject typically drops the interaction to a new low. That's unless someone finds themselves launched, pressured, railroaded, or co-erced into a situation where governance has a modicum of relevance. Maybe you took a chance on this book by picking it up at a garage sale or perhaps it was a Christmas gift from your mother-in-law. However, it's unlikely that you're fulfilling a childhood dream of being a board member. You may have aspired to be a pilot or a firefighter or a doctor or a lawyer or a teacher or a dentist or a Walmart greeter—but not a board member.

After introducing Policy Governance® to a board, I'm periodically asked by attendees why they've never heard some of the things I share or why they weren't told certain things before they joined the board. The implied assumption is that someone else on the board was holding out on them. The greater likelihood is that the blind have been leading the blind.

Suppose you're experiencing some chest pains that feel like indigestion, except they don't go away. Avoiding bad pizza and adding copious amounts of antacid to your diet haven't helped. Eventually the pain is so severe that you end up in the emergency ward where treatment requires open heart surgery. You're prepped, told the risk factors, and eventually loaded onto a stretcher headed for the operating room. It rolls quietly down the hallway as you lie on your back, staring at the ceiling and fighting the anxiety that comes with such invasive surgery. You allow your eyes to wander, which immediately ramps up your anxiety: instead of green scrubs, you discover you're being escorted by someone in a monogrammed shirt with cufflinks. On the other side is a lady in a police uniform, and walking next to her is someone wearing the hat of an airline captain. "What's happening here?" you ask. "Where's the heart surgeon?" You are condescendingly assured that while there's no cardiologist, everyone who's going to be in the operating room is an expert in some field. How long would it take for you get off that stretcher and sprint to the nearest exit, backless gown and all?

This book is for people serving on boards which are loaded with experts: successful businesspeople, doctors, lawyers, and real estate tycoons, but they lack the expertise for the very job they're doing.

If you've spent any amount of time looking into the subject of board governance, you have come across Policy Governance—or what is often referred to as the Carver model, informally named after John Carver who developed the Policy Governance system.

I'm often asked if Policy Governance can be applied effectively in the church context. When Policy Governance, the church, and the Bible are used in the same sentence, someone will rhetorically ask, "But isn't the church different?" This book is written from the perspective that the answer is *yes*. The church is different and the Bible needs to be the final authority as it relates to how a church is led. We understand that God is not a god of disorder, and as such everything should be done in an appropriate and orderly way. It's to that end that we want to see what Policy Governance has to say and how it can contribute to excellence in church governance.

Churches are different. They are different from other faith-based organizations in part because a church's theological and doctrinal beliefs are at the core of what makes a church a church.[1] Churches are relationally different. Unlike many other faith-based organizations, churches are comprised of people who identify a particular church as being *their* church. Those people see themselves as more than corporate members. The church is their spiritual family.

Churches have their history and traditions. Things have been done a certain way for generations. Why would they change what they're used to? Why change what they don't want to change? Even if there was a desire for some change, the pain of change often quashes that desire.

Churches have their polity and bylaws. Structures are in place. Structure, by virtue of its definition, makes change somewhat problematic. It's like a major renovation. The surface changes are often the easiest to accomplish. Once the façade wears off, you encounter unanticipated complications. It's similar with changes to church bylaws; they can be complex and unwieldy, to say nothing of surprising.

Many churches are part of a denomination. The headquarters of the larger affiliation mandates the makeup of the church board, identifies who the chair will be, and requires that certain committees be in place. As much as the local church may want to make changes, the denomination may not permit those changes to even be considered.

As you read this book, you may come across ideas which simply could not be implemented in your church. There may be some load-bearing legal walls that limit certain renovations. Your church family may have done things a certain way for so long that monumental changes would threaten to break it up. You may come to the end of the book and realize that your church is doing quite well under its current structure.

---

[1] Many faith-based mission agencies, camps, schools, and humanitarian organizations have a statement of faith and/or a doctrinal position. However, in the case of a church, that statement or position often generates a degree of passion beyond what is experienced in other faith-based organizations.

So while this book is not intended to cover every ecclesiological contingency, hopefully it will address some overarching principles which can raise the level of your governance proficiency. If you are part of an autonomous church which can make changes to its method of governance, allow yourself to be challenged. Consider how certain changes could be made to free your church to be all it can be.

If the church is the hope of the world, it follows that every effort needs to be made to ensure this hope functions with the greatest efficiency possible to facilitate the greatest effectiveness possible. God is worthy of it, and people are worth it.

Because the church is different, let me invite you to keep some terms in mind.

Later in the book we will look at the one employee who reports to the board. Policy Governance refers to the role filled by that employee as the chief executive officer (CEO). There are various titles used by churches to describe the CEO role. These include minister, senior pastor, and lead pastor. While I'm tempted to use the term CEO, I have decided it may be a hurdle too high for some to clear. Many churches struggle with becoming too businesslike.[2] With a view to minimizing obstacles, I've chosen the commonly used title *pastor*. Feel free to find-and-replace it with the title with which you or your board are most familiar and comfortable.

This isn't meant to be a comprehensive exposition about Policy Governance. John Carver's materials serve as the official source documents. Others more qualified have written on the subject. You can obtain information about these sources in the bibliography at the end of this book.

I'm writing specifically to examine the application of John Carver's Policy Governance system in the context of a local church. You will note that I refer throughout the book to Policy Governance as a *system* rather than a model. The reason is so that you will view Policy Governance as a set of principles. When these principles are integrated in their totality, they provide for a dynamic governing system rather than a sterile model which is just mechanically emulated.

---

[2] I contend that if businesses ran their businesses in the same way many churches run their churches, those businesses would be out of business.

"Church politics" is a dreaded phrase. Your church has enough challenges without them being compounded in the board room. Your church has enough enemies without having them sit across from you in a board meeting—or worse yet, stand behind the pulpit.

My ultimate desire is to provide guidance for those in leadership and governance roles in the church. Hopefully this will lead your board toward excellence in governance for the greatest cause in the world.

1

DOES THIS SOUND LIKE YOUR BOARD?

Some time ago, I was asked to sit on the board of a mission organization. Before I had a chance to say no, I was assured that there were only four meetings a year and that I didn't need to do anything. I politely said, "Nah, that's not really something that interests me."

"But Ted," the recruiter implored, "I need to find two more board members and I can't get anyone to agree. This would really help me out."

So why was it so hard for him to find someone to fill a role that was so important, so easy, and didn't require much time? If it didn't require much time or work, is it possible that it just wasn't all that important? Or is board governance more important than many people understand? Are board members finding out that their positions demand more time than they originally committed to? Maybe it sounded easy at the beginning but has become tough work.

Many board meetings are focused and meaningful. People sit around a table interacting on the future direction of their church. They discuss how their congregation can have a greater impact on their communities. How can the church address some of the needs of families on the same street? How can the ministries of the church assist attendees to grow in their faith?

Just as many church board meetings start by members arriving with a set agenda. The pastor brings forward some plans that require board approval. These plans sound like they will evangelize the city, solve community homelessness, get teens off drugs, and fill the pews. With such noble and ambitious plans, the meeting requires little more than some cursory discussion followed by the board members figuratively pulling out their rubber stamps.

How does it get to be this way? Is that just the way boards work, or are there cultures that contribute to rote board behavior? If it's the latter, how does that change?

If board members come onto a board without an understanding of what their job entails and without any training, it only makes sense that they will tread softly. Better to be thought a fool by the minority than to open one's mouth and prove the minority right. So they sit quietly and watch what others do. The idea that a board will have any discussion about who the church will impact, and what that impact will look like, has never been considered. After all, that's the pastor's job. The board expects the hired expert to come up with a plan and direction. Unless the board doesn't care about people going to heaven or the poor having a home or kids getting off drugs, it assumes that it simply needs to get onside with the plan.

THE IDEA THAT A BOARD WILL HAVE ANY DISCUSSION ABOUT WHO THE CHURCH WILL IMPACT, AND WHAT THAT IMPACT WILL LOOK LIKE, HAS NEVER BEEN CONSIDERED. AFTER ALL, THAT'S THE PASTOR'S JOB.

There is a newbie on the board. She's a young single professional lady who has been voted in by a progressive church as the token representative for the church's women, singles, and young adults. She's too inexperienced and naïve to know better than to ask provoking questions. With the pastor expressing such a clear and compelling vision with passion and vigor, most questions would be rendered somewhere between irrelevant and disrespectful, but she treads where veteran board members fear to tread. "How is our suburban church geographically positioned to effectively care for homeless people? Do we have enough money to pay for the staff to work with troubled teens when our previous motion said we would start a campaign to raise funds for a new console for the pipe organ?" How might we expect the board chair to respond? "Wow, Julie, we're so glad you're on the board to ask these good questions." Or does horrified silence express the board's abhorrence, thus leaving our new board member embarrassed but educated?

Maybe it's better to be passive than actively engage in any kind of meaningful leadership role that adds value to the organization. Board meetings often consist of people sitting around, waiting to vote on an idea that's already been convincingly presented by the pastor. In light of the fact that board members aren't thoroughly versed in the issues, passivity is passed off as wisdom.

When a board responds passively to information it receives, any decisions it's required to make as a result of that information will tend to be reactive rather than proactive. Instead of the board giving proactive consideration to how the church can impact its community, it reacts to whatever is placed in front of it. Of course, there are boards that think they are proactive, convinced that it's their job to set the direction for every detail within an organization. But that's not being proactive; that's micromanaging, but we'll look at that later. I'm talking about those board members who come to a board meeting, fold their arms, wait for the information to be downloaded, and then react subjectively to the information they're given. All that's left to do is raise their right hands a little higher than their elbows.

> WHEN A BOARD RESPONDS PASSIVELY TO INFORMATION IT RECEIVES, ANY DECISIONS IT'S REQUIRED TO MAKE AS A RESULT OF THAT INFORMATION WILL TEND TO BE REACTIVE RATHER THAN PROACTIVE

While we're on the subject of subjectivity, board members are often more subjective than objective. Any input or decision is based on feelings rather than facts. This is demonstrated by responses such as "Sounds good to me" or "I just don't feel comfortable with the idea." When I hear that, I'm not sure what part of a board's anatomy is uncomfortable—and if it was comfortable, what would that feeling be? And in what way is something that "sounds good" better than the alternative? The truth is that the board has no objective reference point for its decision, just subjective comfort or discomfort.

> ...BOARD MEMBERS ARE OFTEN MORE SUBJECTIVE THAN OBJECTIVE

A board will often default to being pragmatic rather than principled. The opposite of principled is not always unprincipled. A board often

A BOARD WILL OFTEN DEFAULT TO BEING PRAGMATIC RATHER THAN PRINCIPLED.

makes decisions based on what works rather than on the basis of any principles. Consideration of items and ideas which are brought forward are based on pragmatism. Determinations are based on what will work or what makes sense rather than coming to the meeting with a clear set of previously developed principles which guide the board's decisions.

Do you ever wonder why your board meetings have to be so long and tedious? One of the reasons is because the default position of the board is permission-withholding rather than permission-granting. You've probably heard people say, "This will require board approval." The assumption is that it's not okay unless the board says it's okay. To make it right, or permissible, requires board approval rather than beginning with an assumption that everything is okay unless a specific limitation has previously been set on a certain activity or action. Boards are afraid that if they don't hold to the default permission-withholding position, things could get out of control.

That concern squeezes the life out of a board trapped between the rocks of micromanagement and rubberstamping. To avoid that dilemma, a board may want to see micromanagement and rubberstamping as two ends of

WHEN A BOARD TWEAKS SOMETHING THAT'S BROUGHT FORWARD BY THE PASTOR, IT'S OFTEN THE BOARD'S WAY OF PREVENTING ITS COLLECTIVE CONSCIENCE FROM FEELING GUILTY OF MICROMANAGING OR RUBBERSTAMPING.

a continuum. No board wants to characterize itself as micromanaging or rubberstamping, because those are considered to be unacceptable terms. So it tries to balance itself on the center point of the continuum by *tweaking*. When a board tweaks something that's brought forward by the pastor, it's often the board's way of preventing its collective conscience from feeling guilty of micromanaging or rubberstamping. If it gets into too many details, it's micromanaging, and that's apparently a bad thing. Rubberstamping, on the other hand, means its role is meaningless. Tweaking usually constitutes some semantic or nonmaterial changes. That becomes the board's way of appeasing its collective conscience.

countries by using carrier pigeons from Switzerland. Rumbold dismissed the report with the note that pigeon post with England "would appear to be almost impossible." PRO, F.O. 371/3379A/ 85819.
23. VSAr, PA, XXVII, Bd. 62.
24. Protocol of the meeting, BBAr, LGS, S. 266.
25. Memorandum by Paravicini, BBAr, LGS, S. 266.
26. BBAr, LGS, S. 266 Balabanova, *My Life*, p. 215.
27. Balabanoff, *My Life*, pp. 215–16.
28. Müller's report to the Bundesrat's secret meeting, November 5, 1918, BBAr, LGS, S. 266.
29. Dutasta's statement was delivered orally; it is reproduced here according to Calonder's account to the Bundesrat. On the same day, November 4, Pageot explained that the danger of Bolshevism in Switzerland had arisen because "the government is weak, the press is without controls, and the right of assembly is absolute." FMA.
30. Protocol, BBAr, LGS, S. 266.
31. Willi Gautschi, *Der Landesstreik 1918* (Zurich, 1968), p. 211.
32. *PSS*, 50:201.

NOTES TO CHAPTER 10
Expulsion

1. The Germans apparently staged the incident with the aim of compromising the Bolshevik embassy in Berlin. See Winfried Baumgart, *Deutsche Ostpolitik 1918* (Vienna, 1966), pp. 358–60.
2. The following discussion of the activity of the Bundesrat is based on the records of the public meetings, to be found in the formal bound book of protocols, BBAr, and on the records of the secret meetings, to be found in the file on Balabanova, BBAr, LGS, S. 266.
3. BBAr, LGS, S. 266; Will Gautschi, *Dokumente zum Landesstreik* (Zurich, 1971), pp. 177–80.
4. Minute on Rumbold's report of Dutasta's actions, November 7, 1918, PRO, F.O. 371/3317/25416.
5. Paul Schmid-Ammann, *Die Wahrheit über den Generalstreik von 1918* (Zurich, 1968), p. 205; Georges Wagnière, *La Suisse et la Grande Guerre* (Lausanne, 1938), pp. 227–33.

If any of this sounds terrifyingly familiar, then you know your board is ready for change. Or is it? If the characteristics we have looked at reflect a deeply rooted culture, then any attempts at change will expose one more challenge, being that a board is typically resilient rather than malleable. In my vernacular, resilience is not a distinguishing feature to be embraced. When something is bent out of its original shape, left alone over time, and eventually returns to its original shape, that's resilience. When I work with boards, the issue of resilience presents the greatest challenge. I'll tell a board that it will need to make some huge changes if it's going to move toward a new model of governing. I go to great lengths to explain what those changes will be and that they will be hard. However, invariably and all too soon a board will demonstrate its resilience by drifting back to the way it has always done business.

If I've described features that you see in your board and if you want to address those challenges, there is hope. There's no need to resign. As we move forward, you'll be equipped with some good questions, as well as some answers to those questions.

2

WHAT IS GOVERNANCE?

Vince Lombardi is considered to be one of the greatest coaches in the history of the National Football League. One reason for that honor was his capacity as a motivator, including his speech about what it takes to be number one: "Winning is not a sometime thing, it's an all the time thing. You don't win once in a while, you don't do things right once in a while, you do them right all the time. Winning is a habit. Unfortunately, so is losing."[3]

Good governance has some of the same characteristics as winning. For a board, good governance is not a sometimes thing; it's an all-the-time thing. You don't govern well once in a while; you govern well all the time. Good governance is a habit. Unfortunately, so is poor governance.

> YOU DON'T GOVERN WELL ONCE IN A WHILE; YOU GOVERN WELL ALL THE TIME. GOOD GOVERNANCE IS A HABIT. UNFORTUNATELY, SO IS POOR GOVERNANCE.

Back to Lombardi. He would start every season by holding up a football and giving his "this is a football" speech.

All the players knew that at the first team meeting, the legendary coach would waste no time getting straight to the point. Many of the men, half Lombardi's age and twice his size, were openly fearful, dreading the encounter. The coach did not disappoint them, and, in fact, delivered his message in one of the great

---

[3] *Thinkexist.com*, "Vince Lombardi quotes." Date of access: March 9, 2015 (http://thinkexist.com/quotation/winning_is_not_a_sometime_thing-it-s_an_all_time/149897.html).

one-liners of all time. Football in hand, Lombardi walked to the front of the room, took several seconds to look over the assemblage in silence, held out the pigskin in front of him, and said, "Gentlemen, this is a football." In only five words, Lombardi communicated his point: We're going to start with the basics and make sure we're executing all the fundamentals.[4]

Legend has it that Max McGee, one of his players, interrupted one of Lombardi's infamous speeches to say, "Coach, could you slow down a little? You're going too fast for us."

Why would a coach recruit professional football players who didn't know what a football was, where the sidelines were, or how to find the end zone? Obviously they knew those fundamental details of football. Maybe he focused on an aspect of life that many of us intuitively know about but forget. Lombardi wanted to remind his players that in the midst of a training camp that would have them puking and include drills that numbed their brains, there was a goal. In the midst of his infamous rants, which left big, grown men cowering in fear, he knew that some players would fail—or bail—if they lost sight of the basics.

So why are you on a governing board? If it's just a volunteer role that someone needs to fill, you'll want to know how short the meetings will be. If you see yourself as being subjected to reading reports that cure insomnia, then the fewer of those reports, the better. But if you can hold the governance football, see the sidelines, and stand in the organizational end zone, you'll be better prepared to engage in the governance game.

Without getting into the etymology of the word governance, its roots are imbedded both literally and figuratively in the idea of steering a ship. It comes from the Latin word *guberno*, which means to steer or pilot. This person isn't the owner or captain of the ship, but rather the one making sure the ship is heading in the right direction.

Governance at virtually every level of society is necessary. Whenever there is a group of people who have a common cause and need leadership to steer them in the right direction, governance is required.

---

[4] *Packerville U.S.A.*, "Gentlemen, this is a football." Date of access: March 2, 2015 (http://packerville.blogspot.ca/2010/05/gentlemen-this-is-football.html).

Suppose, for example, there was a move among your relatives to have a family reunion. There were enough likes on Facebook to know that a large family trip is a common interest. However, we all know this trip will never happen with a hundred people trying to put it together, so a committee is born. This committee essentially governs on behalf of the rest of the family.

This committee isn't the *boss* of the trip. It doesn't get to decide that the trip will be a ferry ride to Martha's Vineyard if the extended family wants to go to Hawaii. It doesn't get to throw down its credit card without having a ballpark idea of how much the extended family is willing to pay. It certainly doesn't have the right to pull down the Facebook page so it doesn't have to listen to whining family members. The committee is the link between the extended family and the travel agent. Note as well that the loyalty of this governing committee is to the family, not to the travel agent. The committee must not authorize the travel agent to book a Mediterranean cruise because that's what the agent likes. Sounds like a no-brainer, right? Hang around some boards and you'll be thankful they aren't governing in the context of your next family reunion.

Every church of any reasonable size requires a group of people to be responsible for taking the intentions of the church and seeing that those intentions are realized. That group is often referred to as a board. The group is made up of members voted in from among the church membership. The idea that they're voted on suggests that the membership is looking for individuals who will see that the church ship is heading in the direction the membership desires.[5]

> GOVERNANCE IMPLIES LEGITIMACY. IT ASSUMES THAT THE GOVERNING BODY—THE BOARD—HAS A LEGITIMATE RIGHT TO GOVERN.

Governance implies legitimacy. It assumes that the governing body—the board—has a legitimate right to govern. It's been voted on or appointed by the people on whose behalf it governs. Back to your family reunion; you want to make sure the people governing on behalf of the family are those the rest of the relatives want. You know what will

---

[5] Later we'll look at the role of elders and how that's different from a governing board.

happen if that isn't the case. *Why is he doing this or that? She's a control freak. It's their idea because they have the money.* Thus it's vital that a board be granted the legitimate right to govern.

Governance implies accountability. A governing board gives fresh meaning to servant leadership. The board is not only appointed *by* those on whose behalf it governs, it serves *on behalf of* those same people. That's why annual member meetings take place. Later on we'll look at what Policy Governance refers to as owner connection. For now, let me say that a board must connect with its members to know what those members want.

Governance implies leadership. It's not in place to react to the initiatives of management. You don't want your family reunion committee to merely react to the ideas of the travel agent. The travel agent must only make arrangements based on the family's preferred destination. In the same way, the board will take the intentions of those who have appointed it and give direction to those wishes.

> CHURCH GOVERNANCE IS THE ROLE OF PROVIDING OVERALL DIRECTION AND CONTROL OF A CHURCH ON BEHALF OF ITS CONSTITUENTS AND ENSURING THAT SUCH DIRECTION AND CONTROL ARE MAINTAINED.

We have looked at examples of poor governance as well as some the characteristics of good governance. But what is church governance? Church governance is the role of providing overall direction and control of a church on behalf of its constituents and ensuring that such direction and control are maintained. What I've referred to as constituents, Policy Governance refers to as legal and moral owners. We will look at this when we attempt to identify who owns the church, but we'll go with this for the purpose of our governance definition for the local church.

Don't worry if you don't know where the sidelines are or which way you're supposed to be going. For now it's sufficient that you know what the governance football is—and what it isn't.

You might be one of those who have a problem hanging onto this governance football. Perhaps your biblical values are such that touching this unclean pigskin is abhorrent to you. In the next chapter, we're going to take a hard look at whether governance, the church, and the Bible can coexist. Please don't put your Bible down while you pick up the governance ball. Put one under each arm as we look at whether or not governance is biblical.

3

IS GOVERNANCE BIBLICAL,
NON-BIBLICAL, OR ABIBLICAL?

"Man prefers to believe what he prefers to be true." So said Sir Francis Bacon, a philosopher of the sixteenth and seventeenth centuries. If his quote is reflective of the truth—although I often prefer it wasn't—then this chapter will be a challenge for both author and reader. Seeing as the subject of this book has to do with governance within the context of the local church, let's see if there is any biblical basis for it.

Dr. Larry Perkins points out,

> Within Paul's discussion of the grace-gifts provided by the Holy Spirit to disciples of Christ we find the term *kubernēsis*, translated in the NIV as "administration" (1 Corinthians 12:28). It is not clear exactly what ability Paul is defining through this term. Many English versions link this term with 'administration'.... A cognate noun *kubernētēs* occurs in Acts 27:11 and Revelation 18:17. NIV renders this noun as "pilot" in Acts and as "sea captain" in Revelation. Both contexts refer to a person in charge of a ship... Given that deity often has the responsibility to "govern, direct, steer" the universe, it should come as no surprise that one of the "gifts" that the Holy Spirit supplies to Christ's church would be kubernēsis, i.e. the act of serving as helmsman and piloting the church safely and carefully. Further, its association with state governance, i.e. the rule of kings, indicates that it means more than merely "administration," i.e. management. There lies within this word a more fundamental

responsibility, an equipping for governance. It should come as no surprise that this Greek term etymologically forms the basis for our English words "govern, governance."[6]

To this point, we're on safe ground in concluding that the gift of governance is found in the New Testament, noting that the only reference to it is in 1 Corinthians 12:28. This gift is listed in the context of Paul's challenge to the church in Corinth, that each individual in the church has a special part in the body of Christ. He doesn't expand on how this gift is to be used, only that it is a gift that *can* be used.

In the next chapter, we'll look at the role of elders in the church. For now let's note that there is no biblical foundation for believing the governance gift—*kubernēsis*—is linked to that of an elder, bishop, pastor, or deacon. Any time those roles are addressed, the requirements are that of character and passion, along with some aptitudes. To link the gift of governance to that of the calling to be an elder, bishop, pastor, or deacon would force an interpretation where the scriptures make no such connection.

Having established that the gift of governance exists, we need to discern whether there's a biblical foundation for the use of this governance gift in the church, within the context of our earlier definition of governance. Keep in mind that we aren't questioning the need for leadership in the church. Spiritual leaders are necessary, as we'll see in the next chapter. The question is whether the New Testament prescribes a governance structure at all.

As early as Acts 6:2, we get a description of how the apostles delegated some of the practical ministries of the church so they could devote themselves to the study and teaching of the scriptures. However, there seems to be no instruction which allows for the church body to identify a governing group who will act on its behalf. Nowhere in the New Testament do we see that adherents of a church had any democratic input regarding the church's vision. There's no mention of the idea that a local body of Christians could determine why their particular church

---

[6] Dr. Larry Perkins, "The Gift of Governance," *Internet Moments with God's Words*. Date of access: March 2, 2015 (http://moments.nbseminary.com/archives/2012/02/).

existed in contradistinction to another church. The only thing we know is that the gift of governance existed and that the demonstration of that gift does not appear to be described.

So if the Bible is silent on the matter of governance in the church, maybe there's no place for it. Let's get rid of it and see what that looks like.

Suppose the elders of a church were the sole leaders, with the exclusive prerogative and responsibility for leadership. If they wanted to relocate the church, it would be their call. If they wanted to hire staff, it would be up to them. They would control the expenditures, and arguably they could control the income by setting a membership fee at whatever level they felt was necessary to cover their self-determined expenses. It would be essentially *their* church. While there are undoubtedly churches where such is the case, I think it's safe to assume they won't be reading this book. Leaders in a church where there's no governance accountability to the congregation will be quick to point out that it's God's church and their position is to oversee *His* church. However, the governance point has been sidestepped. If it's God's church, then what is their legitimacy for their role as elders?

In Acts 20:28, Paul reminds the elders at the church in Ephesus that the Holy Spirit made them elders. However, they were likely the very first elders in a church that was in its infancy. The same applies to the churches in Crete, where Paul tells Titus to appoint elders (Titus 1:5). Many or all of the church adherents would have been new believers and obviously looking for outside direction. Those churches didn't have the scriptures such as we have them today to guide them in their choice of elders. Even as Paul described the characteristics of elders, he acknowledged the need for legitimacy. He was clear that they couldn't lead the house of God if they couldn't demonstrate leadership credibility in their own homes.

> LEADERSHIP MUST ALWAYS HAVE LEGITIMACY. THE ONLY ALTERNATIVE TO LEADERSHIP WITH LEGITIMACY IS LEADERSHIP BY TYRANNY.

Leadership must always have legitimacy. The only alternative to leadership with legitimacy is leadership by tyranny. In other words, "I'm the leader because I say so and you don't have the power to stop me."

If the elders are the spiritual leaders of the church, there must be some way of legitimizing that leadership other than by self-appointment, self-perpetuation, or a posture that says, "God told me; how dare you question Him?"

So back to our original question: is governance, as we are defining it, biblically required, unbiblical and to be avoided, or abiblical, and as such not addressed in the Bible?

Church governance as we understand it today wasn't conceived of in the first-century church. The church didn't typically own property, file government returns, or set up bank accounts. So while the concept of governance as we see it now is not biblical, there is nothing to suggest it contradicts anything in the Bible. I propose that a congregationally accountable governing board is abiblical; that is, nothing in the Bible speaks to it one way or the other. However, I would offer that governance and leadership legitimacy are two ways of increasing the likelihood of order, which is itself a biblical concept.

So far we have identified the characteristics of some traditional boards and arrived at an understanding of what governance is. We have decided that congregationally accountable governance is a good thing for the local church. We did this while assuming that elders have a vital but separate role as leaders in the church. In the next chapter, we will discover how these roles are separate and compatible.

4

WHAT'S THE DIFFERENCE
BETWEEN ELDERS AND BOARD MEMBERS?

Given the theme of this book, the matter of biblical elders in contradistinction to governing board members needs to be addressed. With this in mind, I spent a protracted period of time coming up with definitions to describe each role. The phrases ranged from cute to complicated, but never clear or complete. I decided to move onto something easier. How would I compare a car to a cabbage? Soon I realized that distinguishing a car from a cabbage is more about contrast than comparison. Ah, so that's why I was having such a hard time. I was endeavoring to compare two roles that are so different that they are better contrasted than compared.

As we contrast these two roles, I'll make reference to guardians and trustees. Lest these terms be seen as synonymous, let me distinguish them for the purposes of this subject. We understand the idea of a guardian. Typically it's someone who is charged with looking after the interests of someone else—often a minor—who doesn't have the life experience, expertise, or capacity to look after themselves. The minor doesn't get to decide where they will live or go to school. Someone else has that prerogative. On the other hand, a trustee typically serves at the pleasure of the individual or group.

So how is the role of an elder different than that of a board member?

The first obvious difference—like, you *drive* a car and *eat* a cabbage—is that the concept of elders is based in scripture while that of a board member is a much more modern idea. We discovered in the last chapter that the Bible doesn't give clear direction as to how a church is governed. However, to maintain leadership legitimacy, some form of congregationally accountable governance is required.

The elder in a New Testament church has a variety of roles, all of which center on the spiritual and doctrinal health of the church. An elder is charged with maintaining a firm grip on biblical truth so it can be taught. Beyond that, an elder has the responsibility of rebutting and rebuking those who oppose the truth (Titus 1:9). This is consistent with the solemn mandate of church leaders who have a God-given responsibility so immense that God will hold them accountable for how they have watched over the church (Hebrews 13:17). When that time comes, the writer to the Hebrew Christians says it would be for the good of both the leader and his or her followers if the leader could give account with joy. That sounds ominously like the instructions given to one's kids in the presence of a babysitter: "You better be in bed by nine o'clock. When I get home, I'll be asking her if you were in bed, and if I find out you weren't, that will be a bad thing."

There are theological matters and doctrinal interpretations which are not up for debate among board members. Church meetings shouldn't be held to vote on the core doctrinal values of the church. We don't have the right to argue with elders because we suddenly see certain passages of scripture in a new light. Elders must not poll the church to find out what members think about certain fundamental issues. This is based on the statement in Acts 20:28 that it is the Holy Spirit who gives elders the responsibility to watch over the congregation.

THE GOVERNING BOARD OF A CHURCH HAS THE ROLE OF A TRUSTEE RATHER THAN A GUARDIAN.

By contrast, the board as a group serves on behalf of, and is accountable to, the members of the church. It listens to the members and acts on their behalf, ensuring that their informed wishes are carried out. The governing board of a church has the role of a trustee rather than a guardian.

The local church is much more complex than the church in the first century. Back then, a church community typically met in a home, although records show that some churches met in Jewish temples. The church was new, and as such elders were appointed by church planters.

While we don't know how many elders were in each church, according to Acts 14:23 and Titus 1:5 there was clearly more than one.

Most churches today meet in buildings with a capacity much larger than that of a first-century home. The ease of transportation makes it convenient for people to come from longer distances, allowing for churches to be much larger. After all, how far would you want to ride your donkey or walk, as many still do today in other countries? Add to this an additional level of complexity that comes with churches registering as charities.

How then do these two groups of leaders—board members and elders—coexist? What if they're in conflict? Who gets to decide what?

If we eliminate the role of elders, we have an organization that is ultimately ruled by the members of the church. Conversely, the fact that a church is registered as a charity means that it *is* ultimately ruled by its members. Members get to vote on who will be on the board. This means that church members can democratically change their statement of faith so that whatever fancies the majority can be added or deleted.[7] While this is a legal possibility, it's an abandonment of the scriptural intent for having elders.

A church must acknowledge that those within the church who have a guardianship role must be honored. Elders have the role of looking after the interests of those of us who do not have the spiritual experience, biblical insights, or doctrinal acumen to look after our own interests. Elders must be seen as sacrosanct in a way that doesn't subject them to the electoral process or rationale of expediency.

> A CHURCH MUST ACKNOWLEDGE THAT THOSE WITHIN THE CHURCH WHO HAVE A GUARDIANSHIP ROLE MUST BE HONORED.

If you've been on a church board, you're aware that the time mostly gets eaten up by administrative minutia. The first-century church had a similar problem, for which the apostles came up with a solution: they appointed people who would make sure the administrative details were taken care of, so they could focus their time and attention on the ministry of teaching God's Word. Many modern church boards haven't done this, so when

---

[7] This may not apply to churches which have a Presbyterian or Episcopalian structure.

practical details go head to head with the study of the Bible, you can guess which one gets the most attention.

One of the ways to deal with this problem is to do the same thing as the church did in Acts 6. Start by divvying up the responsibilities, leaving the elders to stay focused on their God-given call and not be required to sit at the boardroom table. Elders shouldn't be expected to deal with issues of administration, accounting, programming, parking lot maintenance, or staff salaries. Nor should they become involved in vision-setting and strategic planning. Their role is to ensure the vision, planning, and programming are biblically consistent.

The board, on the other hand, will listen to the congregation to address other issues. Does the church want to reach its immediate community or should it seek to reach the entire city? Is it clear what the spiritual results will be in the lives of those who attend? To which socioeconomic group does the membership sense it has a responsibility? Will only spiritual needs be met or will the results of the church ministry include physical and social needs? Has consideration been given to the impact on those who may not otherwise be reached? These are details unique to each church. They aren't doctrinal or theological, nor do they affect the spiritual health of the church.

There's no overlap in the role of elders in relation to the role of the board. The potential for conflict comes when elders begin to slide from their role as the guardians of spiritual and doctrinal integrity of the church and begin dealing in matters which aren't doctrinally specific. At the same time, the board needs to be careful to ensure that nothing is allowed to take place which would compromise or undermine the spiritual leadership of the elders.

It is vital that the board underscores the important role and work of the elders. The authority of the elders must be acknowledged so they can ensure that the theological and doctrinal positions of the church are being adhered to.

Individual board members can only speak to issues in the context of a board meeting, and the voice of the board will be heard as a motion that has been passed. You'll notice that I've not referred to a *board of elders*. While elders need to speak with one voice as they put forward stated positions, individual elders can and should speak as individuals from time to time. If someone in the church is struggling with a personal issue or decision and looking for counsel from an elder, it is reasonable to expect that the elder won't share those details with other elders. An exception to this would be if specific permission is granted for it to be shared or there's a legal reason to disclose.

It's clear from the Bible that an elder has a special calling and responsibility. That being so, it's hard to envision that they have a calling on their life for a three-year term that ends at midnight December 31. Board members, on the other hand, can have terms which are outlined in the bylaws.

So let's contrast these two roles.[8]

- Elders are charged, whereas board members are democratically elected.

- Elders rule on theological and doctrinal issues, whereas board members represent and rule on organizational matters.

- Elders serve as guardians of theological and doctrinal issues, whereas board members serve as trustees to oversee the church's ability to carry out its distinctive mission.

- Elders function in a role that has been given to them by the Holy Spirit, whereas board members act on behalf of the desire of the congregation.

- Elders continue in their role until they are not able or willing, whereas board members serve for a defined period of time.

So this really is cars and cabbages.

Although we will focus on the governance role of the board, we do so while acknowledging the biblical role of elders.

---

[8] While these are two separate roles, some would suggest that they can and should be carried out by the same group of people. While I agree that both roles can be carried out by the same body, I recommend that having two different bodies helps to keep the roles separate and allows for individuals to maximize their specific gifts, aptitudes, and capacities.

Now that we've described the type of board you may be used to, and distinguished governance from guardianship, we will now look at the Policy Governance system to see how it can be applied in the context of the twenty-first-century local church.

5

WHAT IS
POLICY GOVERNANCE®?

I'm not overly fond of pie, but I love the filling—unless it's rhubarb, which tastes like vegetated battery acid. Lemon meringue, on the other hand, is to die for. The part I don't like is the crust. I've tried unsuccessfully to imagine a type of food described as *crust* that might taste good. Crust is the vegetarian counterpart to *scab*. My ninety-two-year-old mother-in-law still bakes pies, including lemon meringue—and she came up with a creative way of getting her special son-in-law to enjoy her pie. When the rest of the family is sentenced to eating the cardboard with the lemon meringue, she makes me a special pie without the crust. She serves it in a dish the way pie should be served—and yes, it's to die for.

I've tried in vain to point out to my wife Lorna that her mother has learned the secret to baking good pies. Lorna points out that what I'm served is not lemon meringue *pie*, but rather lemon meringue *pudding*. She contends that it's the filling inside the crust that makes it a pie. Lemon meringue pie isn't merely a combination of the ingredients. Mixing the lemon, the meringue, and the crust and tossing it into a pie plate doesn't constitute lemon meringue pie. The crust goes on the bottom, the filling goes in the middle, and the meringue goes on top. Lemon meringue pie is *something*, and it is apparently *not* whatever I'd like it to be.

We started out by defining governance and making the case for the necessity of congregationally accountable governance. Now we're going to look at one particular system of governance that has simultaneously gained a great deal of endorsement and notoriety over the past few decades. Our intention in this book is to see how this system can be applied in a local church context without violating the biblical values of a typical evangelical church.

Many organizations, and even some churches, will tell you that they use a hybrid version of Policy Governance. In fact, if they were writing this chapter, they likely would not capitalize Policy Governance. After all, like the term governance which I defined, they would maintain that one definition of Policy Governance may be as good as the next. If my definition of governance is categorically wrong, that's not because any one individual or body has the right to say so. It is more likely because the collective body of governance experts would agree that Ted Hull's definition is off.

There's no such thing as a hybrid version of Policy Governance. Like lemon meringue pie, Policy Governance is *something*. It's *not* whatever anyone, or even the collective body of governance experts, wants it to be. The *policy* in Policy Governance is not just an adjective to describe governance. One of the things you may have noted is that Policy Governance is capitalized and there is an ® symbol after the first use of the term in this book. This symbol means that the term Policy Governance is a registered service mark. An individual or business will often use a service mark to distinguish their service from other similar services. In this case, it informs people like you and me who are interested in governance about the source of this governance system.

> THERE'S NO SUCH THING AS A HYBRID VERSION OF POLICY GOVERNANCE.

In the 1980s, John Carver was looking for information regarding the specific role and responsibilities of a board of directors, including the role of a board in relation to its CEO. Out of a dearth of information on the subject, he developed the Policy Governance system. The Policy Governance service mark is owned by John Carver.[9] He and his co-

---

[9] That's why you'll see articles which reference some of the principles of Policy Governance footnoted as follows: "Policy Governance® is an internationally registered service mark of John Carver." While the service mark is owned by John Carver, he and Miriam Carver are the authoritative source.

consultant and partner Miriam Carver are the authoritative source of Policy Governance. Using our lemon meringue analogy, they get to decide the ingredients and how they fit together. However, John Carver didn't come up with some unique governance principles so that he can corner and control the market. Anyone can implement the system; there aren't any license fees or royalties involved.

However, in order to protect the integrity of the principles, the Carvers do require those persons they have directly trained through the Policy Governance® Academy^{SM} to use the service mark. If people like me don't point you in the direction of the authoritative source, Policy Governance has the potential to become whatever anyone says it is or wants it to be. It will be another example of the game we played in school where one person whispers a phrase to the person

> ...THE CARVERS ALONE HAVE THE RIGHT TO STATE WHAT POLICY GOVERNANCE IS—AND IS NOT.

next to them and the hearer passes on what they've heard to the next person. We discovered that what the person at the end of the line said was radically different to what was said by the person who originated the statement. We would agree that the authoritative voice regarding the accuracy of the statement is the student who originally said it, not the person at the end of the line. In the same way, the Carvers alone have the right to state what Policy Governance is—and is not.

I will make every effort to ensure that any reference I make to Policy Governance, including how it applies to churches, is consistent with the principles established by John Carver. The official principles of Policy Governance can be found in Appendix A.

You may have looked at the Policy Governance principles in other books, such as those listed in the bibliography at the end of this book, and found some of the ingredients particularly tasty to the palate of your board. There's nothing preventing you from taking some of the components and applying them to your board. But Policy Governance is not a buffet of best practices that one randomly puts on their governance plate and takes to their board table. It doesn't work like that. You either have Policy Governance in its entirety or you don't have it at all.

Let's say that for $140 a year, you can get a credit card. Along with this card come travel health coverage, trip cancellation insurance, and a myriad of other benefits. The agents for the credit card company will try to convince you that these advantages are indispensable to a discerning traveler. However, you may have travel health insurance through your employer. If so, try telling the commission salesperson at the airport kiosk that you don't need the travel health coverage. You might even try asking if they can reduce the annual fee, as you don't need one of the accessories. It's frustrating if you need some of the benefits but are forced to buy them all.

Policy Governance is different. It's not a list of best practices with a bunch of governance tips added in, some of which you may not need or want. Rather it's a set of integrated principles. Once you pull one of those principles out, Policy Governance is no longer Policy Governance. As we move forward, we'll look at the pieces and see how they fit together.

If this idea goes against your grain, you are not alone. I start most of my do-it-yourself, can-be-assembled-in-fifteen-minutes, no-tools-required projects by grabbing the pieces that look like they should fit together and keep going until it doesn't work. Then my voice gets louder as I graphically express my frustration. When it comes to Policy Governance, I'm always curious as to which parts my well-meaning governance friends want to leave in the box. Often the reason they want to leave parts in the box is because they don't understand the system and what it's intended to do.

If you want to look at customer reviews of Policy Governance, you don't have to look far to find that some organizations have tried it and found it wanting. In every case I've heard about, the breakdown came when one or more of the principles weren't applied. Those pieces are in the box for a reason. If we don't know the reason for a particular piece, one option is to leave it in the box. A second option is to read the authoritative instructions listed in the bibliography at the end of this book.

Before you sit down at the table and dig into the Policy Governance pie, it's important to be clear about what you have ordered. It will be like nothing you have ever tasted before. It's an acquired taste. It doesn't taste like cotton candy that dissolves in your mouth and assaults your pancreas. It has the right ingredients that, when mixed properly, will result in a well-governed church. Having spent time studying and applying Policy Governance in the context of local churches, I'm confident that it can be used effectively and biblically. I'm equally as confident that if it isn't implemented well, it will have the same appeal to a board as rhubarb pie has to me.

6

WHO OWNS
YOUR CHURCH?

It took a whole chapter to say that Policy Governance is *something* as opposed to *anything* anyone wants it to be. Let's now look specifically at one of the principles that makes up Policy Governance: organizational ownership.

So who owns your church? The theologically correct answer is God. To suggest anything else will have me branded as a heretic and wipe out any credibility I may have. Certainly within the biblical understanding of the church, that's true. However, such an exclusive definition poses some twenty-first-century challenges.

The board chair of a small church in Canada contacted me. His board had become increasingly frustrated with the government's involvement in the church. Reports needed to be filed, every dollar needed to be accounted for, and money couldn't be sent to just anyone the church wanted to support. The board felt it would be so much easier if the church wasn't a registered charity.

"So what do we need to do to get out of this?" the chair asked me.

"Nothing," I replied rather flippantly. "Don't file the proper documents and you will be deregistered in short order."

I'm glad he didn't just say thanks and hang up on me, because the answer required more context than I had glibly provided.

"What will you do with the building?" I asked as a follow-up question.

He had been under the impression that the church could just deregister in the same way one could allow a license to expire. The plan to follow my advice took a sharp turn when I informed him that the building was owned by the charity and would need to be sold and the profits given to another registered charity. The church body would need to start over from scratch.

When you refer to the local church in the context of the Bible, you will be accurately referring to it as a local expression of the body of Christ. However, you and I both know that telling a bank manager, a utility provider, or a government authority that God owns the church—and they can collect from Him—isn't going to fly. When you refer to your church by the name on the outside of the building, the concept of ownership is different. It's not only different from the biblical teaching of divine ownership, it's different from the way in which one typically thinks of ownership. We're used to the idea of ownership coming along with assets such as property, shares in a company, or a vehicle. We can take these assets and convert them to cash, which can then be used as we please. The board chair to whom I referred earlier discovered that the church's assets, such as property, could not be sold and the profits distributed to the members. If the church was dissolved as a registered charity, the assets would need to be disposed of and the revenue given to another registered charity.

For many businesses, the owners are easy to identify. They are the ones who own shares. If I own just one share in a bank or an oil company, I'm an owner. And unless I have non-voting shares, I have a say at the annual general meeting and any special general meetings in between. When it comes to charities, those owners can sometimes be much more difficult to identify. But it can—and must—be done.

In the case of a church, it will be clear that the members of the church are the legal owners. The legal owners are the members who attend the annual general meeting (AGM), elect board members, make changes to the bylaws or statement of faith, and appoint the auditor. They're the people who can ultimately shut down the church should they so choose.

The AGM is usually attended by a small fraction of the members. Often these members have been around a long time and their tenure goes back to a bygone era of regular congregational meetings and denominational loyalty. However, there are often many non-members who would consider that particular church to be their home church. They attend regularly, volunteer, and donate, and some might actually think they are members. Different churches will have different terms to describe this group of people, terms such as constituents or adherents. Regardless of the term used, there's typically a mutual acknowledgement between these individuals and the church that this is *their* church. This acknowledgment can even be informal. They may qualify because they have a mailbox in the foyer of the church or their name is in the church directory. They own the mission of the church and are on board with the vision laid out by the pastor. Policy Governance would refer to these people as moral owners to whom those who govern the church are accountable. It is imperative that a church board wrestle with who its owners are, because in the end it's that group of owners on whose behalf the board is governing.

A number of years ago, our son Brian and his wife Theresa decided they would teach overseas for a couple of years. Not willing to burn any bridges, they put much of their furniture in storage. After a few years, they realized that the value of hanging onto their furniture wasn't worth the cost of the storage and thus they had a garage sale.

One of their daughters spied the rocker that had been used to rock her to sleep as a baby.

"You're not selling this!" she pronounced. After being told that it was going to be sold and she needed to get over it, the situation escalated. "How can you do this? You're ruining my life!"

Her mom and dad got a firsthand introduction to the concept of moral ownership. Mom and Dad legally owned the rocking chair. On the one hand, they could do whatever they wanted with it, but they came to the clear realization that there was a broader constituency— their daughter, who believed she had the right to be heard. Decisions were being made that affected her. In fact, her whole life could be ruined by this ill-considered decision.

While the analogy has some loopholes, hopefully you're getting the idea of moral ownership. There are people who make up a church who legitimately anticipate that they'll be listened to. They assume decisions about targeting a particular demographic which to this point has not been targeted, a refocusing exercise, or a relocation initiative will have their input.

So is the Policy Governance concept of ownership just another word for stakeholders? Let's see. Our son did a good job of keeping us informed about his plans to live overseas. Having our granddaughters living three minutes away and realizing that the three-minute drive would become a twenty-four-hour flight through nine zones meant we were stakeholders in their decision. We would be affected if they moved. However, while they knew there would be negative implications for Lorna and me, we didn't get to weigh in on their decision. We were stakeholders, but we were under no illusion that we had any moral ownership.

When it comes to the rocking chair, I was under no illusion that I was a moral owner. Because I was not deemed to be a moral owner, I had no input into the decision whether to keep the rocking chair or put it on Kijiji. The fact that it ended up in my basement only makes me a stakeholder.

In the same way, it is clear that there are people who need to be listened to as it relates to whom the church exists to benefit and what those benefits will be. We'll look at this in more depth later.

The Policy Governance system assumes owner-accountable governance. Because a board governs on behalf of its owners, it must therefore be accountable to its owners. This means more than just issuing an annual report. A board which is owner-accountable will listen to the values of its owners and reflect those values as it governs.

The owners don't benefit from ownership other than the soul-satisfying blessing of knowing the positive difference the church makes in the lives of others.[10] This principle of ownership should exponentially ramp up the responsibility of any board that serves on behalf of its legal and moral owners.

---

[10] In the case of corporations, cooperatives, and trade associations, it's common for a board to determine that the owners are the beneficiaries of the organization. That is not typically the case with charities.

7

IF THE WORD BOARD IS SINGULAR, WHY IS IT REFERRED TO IN THE PLURAL?

Church structure is often laden with committees. There may well be committees for missions, Sunday school, member care, adult ministry, finances, seniors, kitchen, singles, personnel, families, facilities, and outreach. If everyone in the church isn't on a committee, another one will be created. These committees have a chair who sits on the church board as a representative of his or her committee. After a committee has hammered out a recommendation, it goes to the board for approval. The board then begins to carve up the idea, adding its own opinions, and tells the committee chair to take the recommendation back to the committee.

Somewhere in the midst of these committees there may be a pastor or other staff member who has long since lost any understanding of who they report to. The pastor receives a suggestion from one person and an edict from another. A staff person is told one thing by the pastor and another thing from the vice-chair of the singles committee. Many voices with many ideas simultaneously coming from many directions.

Board holism is one of the key principles of Policy Governance. It's the antithesis of the committee-heavy church. If you've sat on a church board but the Policy Governance system is new to you, brace yourself for something radically different than anything you've experienced before. The principle of board holism views the board as an *it* rather than a *them*

> THE PRINCIPLE OF BOARD HOLISM VIEWS THE BOARD AS AN *IT* RATHER THAN A *THEM* OR A GROUP OF BOARD MEMBERS.

or a group of board members. After all, it's the board as a whole which is accountable to its owners.

A board characterized by board holism will have a voice. It will speak with clarity. What it says will not be contradictory. It won't send mixed or conflicting messages—unlike the board we described at the beginning of the chapter. It starts with a common agreement about how a message will be decided and delivered. An example of this is Robert's Rules of Order. One person puts a potential message in the form of a statement and a second person agrees that what the first person said is something worth discussing. The other people around the board table speak to the statement by discussing why it is or isn't a good statement. Eventually the group votes on whether this will be the statement of the board. If a majority agrees, the message becomes the voice of the board. You likely understand it better as a motion that's passed or defeated.

However, suppose you found out some time later that the chair or one of the board members ignored the result of the vote and spoke out or acted based on their own personal preference. You might be surprised and perplexed, but I suspect shock and outrage would better describe your response. You might be thinking, *We discussed this as a board and voted on it, so that's the decision. How does someone get to overrule or ignore that decision?* The answer is simple. Someone isn't buying into the principle of board holism.

Let me digress for a moment. While we often make reference to boards being sued, the fact is that a board cannot be sued. Only individual members of a board are sued. The terrifying fact is that you as a board member can be sued for the actions or inactions of the board.[11] So we want to be sure that when a decision is made, it's the board that has made that decision and not some renegade. You certainly don't want to be implicated by the random decision of a board member who jumps offside.

I knew you'd like the idea of board holism. If you didn't agree with that principle, you would be accepting that individuals on the board have an authority independent of that held by the board as a whole.

---

[11] There are legal and technical nuances which would reduce or remove individual liability for a board decision, but we won't go into them here.

Periodically I'm asked how board holism—the board being an *it* with one clear voice—aligns with idea of the working board. To make sure I understand the question—actually, to make sure *they* understand the question—I may ask someone who uses the term "working board" to clarify what they mean.

"We're a working board," they say. "For example, someone heads up congregational care and someone else oversees building maintenance."

Before they go further, I interrupt. "Whoa, stop… I'm confused. Let me clarify my understanding of what you mean by a working board. You used the word *board* and *someone*. Do those two words mean the same thing?" What I'm trying to discern is whether they see the difference between their board as an *it* compared to the individuals sitting on the board. While diversity is a good thing for board deliberation, once a board decision has been made by due process it should be upheld by all who participated in the process.

Maybe you're on the board of a church like the one we described earlier where board members are assigned certain tasks. Someone on the board oversees the visitation ministry of the church; someone else looks after the Sunday school; a third person serves as the church bookkeeper. Board holism doesn't provide for a working board. A board doesn't typically do member visitation. Someone who happens to sit on the board may volunteer to visit church members, but unless the entire board goes and visits someone, you don't have a working board.

A board has a legal and fiduciary responsibility to make sure the financial records of the church are complete and accurate, but a board doesn't sit around a table and collectively input numbers. The board doesn't gather on Sunday mornings to superintend the children's ministry. Hopefully you see that it's vital to see an individual's role as a ministry volunteer as separate from their role as a board member.

Here's the challenge. When a board member—I mean a congregational care volunteer—brings their report to the board, in what role do they bring it? Are they submitting their report as the congregational care volunteer with their right hand and receiving it as a board member with their left hand? They have to be one or the other, a board member or a congregational care volunteer. They can change roles; however, both the individual and everyone else at the meeting needs to be clear what role is being occupied at any given point in time.

If one doesn't subscribe to the principle of board holism, the role of a board member is not only confusing, it can become dangerous. There is the potential for a board member to go offside by carrying out an action because they believe they have the authority to do so by virtue of being a board member, regardless of whether that action reflects the formal value and voice of the rest of the board members. Or suppose a certain government filing is assumed to be the responsibility of the treasurer. If it's not submitted, the treasurer is on the hook, right? Wrong. The board will be held collectively responsible.

So you have a choice to make. If you don't embrace board holism, including the principle that the board is collectively responsible for its decisions and expresses its decisions with one voice, then like when Israel didn't have one voice at the top, everyone will do that which is right in their own eyes. But if you believe in board holism, and also believe in the working board concept, then the work of the board must be done by the board as a whole. You can't have it both ways.

But there is a solution.

8

WHAT'S THE BOARD'S RESPONSIBILITY?

We started off by defining governance as the role of providing overall direction and control of a church on behalf of its moral owners and ensuring that such direction and control is maintained. We discovered that the role of a board member is different than that of an elder. Then we looked at a couple of Policy Governance principles that distinguish a board that uses Policy Governance from the kind of church board you may be used to. One of those principles is that of church ownership and the importance of a board being able to identify who the owners are. A second principle is that of board holism, seeing the board as an *it*. The individuals on the board have the right to govern because they have been appointed or elected by the owners they represent.

Very early on, we came to the sad conclusion that many people who serve on a board have little or no idea what they're supposed to do. There's often no orientation, in part because there's no one with the knowledge or expertise to provide that orientation. So how are board members supposed to know what they don't know if they don't know what they don't know?

Recently I asked a group of people to identify the board of their church. They had trustees, council members, and an operations committee. They weren't sure if one or all of the groups comprised the board. I pointed out that the answer was easy to obtain. If there was an allegation of child abuse in the church's Sunday school, who would be sued? I assured them that the lawyers would find out who is governing. The reason I go nuclear when the question is asked is because it expedites getting an answer. It assists the church in discovering who makes up this heretofore nebulous and invisible board. The board as a whole needs to ensure that nothing illegal happens and that all the items which are legally required, such as government filings, are taken care of.

I had my previous book, *A Guide to Governing Charities*, reviewed by a lawyer. As we chatted over lunch, he mentioned that it was good that I didn't state everything board members could be held accountable for or no one would want to volunteer. While he acknowledged that his statement was somewhat hyperbolic, it underscored that board members need to understand their responsibilities. For example, in some jurisdictions, if staff is not paid, board members jointly and severally can be legally required to cover those salaries. ("Jointly and severally" essentially means that everyone on the board will be named in a lawsuit, and if there's a judgement, money will be squeezed out of anyone and everyone until the judgement is satisfied.)

If you hang around boards long enough, you'll hear the term *fiduciary* in the context of a board's responsibility. This is a fancy legal term which means a board is responsible to take care of something that has been entrusted to it. This is illustrated when I give money to my financial advisor to invest on my behalf. It's not his money, so he doesn't get to invest it any way he wants. I tell him about my financial goals and my risk tolerance and direct him to take care of my money in a way that's consistent with my overall wishes. In the case of the church, the owners entrust the advancement and protection of the church to a board. They assume that the board will ensure the pastor leads the church in the direction the owners want it to go. This includes such things as making sure that donations are accurately recorded, the building is protected from irrecoverable loss, and employees are paid.

Once board members begin to get a handle on the expanse of their responsibilities, their tendency is to wade into the details. After all, if the board is responsible, it better make sure it controls everything. But how can a board control everything? How can it make sure the staff is paid if it doesn't write the checks—or at least sign them? If members of the board can be sued because someone makes an accusation of abuse, shouldn't board members be in the nursery? No wonder someone on the board needs to be the church treasurer; that role shouldn't be covered by some volunteer. If the board is ultimately responsible, it better take control.

While that sounds ideal, it simply isn't practical. In fact, we have inadvertently compounded the problem. By eliminating the idea of a working board—which is essentially individual board members performing various tasks, and engaging the principle of board holism— we require everyone to do everything.

"Great!" I hear you say. "In just a few chapters, you've moved me from being a board member who just needed to show up for a few meetings a year to now potentially losing my house and kids."[12] You now have all this responsibility that you can't get your arms around, but you can be sued if one of those responsibilities gets dropped or falls through a crack.

We started off by asking what the board's responsibility was. By now you may be wishing you didn't know, or perhaps you're wondering how to get off the board. You're all too aware that if there's a problem, someone is going to come after the members of the board. You aren't buying the suggestion that the responsibility of the board can be delegated to someone. "It's not my fault; I told them to take care of it; go see—or sue them" doesn't sound like it will be well-received.

And you're right.

---

[12] I know, some days losing your kids might seem like an incentive to serve on a board, but we won't go there.

9

HOW CAN A BOARD DELEGATE AUTHORITY WITHOUT GIVING AWAY RESPONSIBILITY?

A t the end of the previous chapter, we had a problem. We learned that the board is responsible for everything that goes on—and goes wrong—in the church. The obvious solution is to control everything. But how does a board do that without micromanaging? Let's see if we can get a handle on this responsibility thing.

The terms responsibility and authority are often used interchangeably without a healthy appreciation for the difference. To start, we need to differentiate the two terms.

You're actually more familiar with the difference than you may think. For instance, at the end of the year you have the option to complete your own tax return or gather up your tax documents and take them to an accountant. The problem with doing it yourself is that you aren't quite sure—or have no idea—what to do. Nevertheless, you and you alone have the responsibility to file your tax return. You cannot offload or delegate that responsibility to someone else,

> ...WHILE YOU CANNOT DELEGATE YOUR *RESPONSIBILITY*, YOU CAN DELEGATE YOUR *AUTHORITY*.

including a qualified CPA. You'll discover this truth in the event the person to whom you thought you had delegated the responsibility doesn't complete your tax return. Try telling the tax department that you delegated it to a CPA and that the tax department can deal with them. You will be reminded that it's your return and that you're ultimately responsible. But while you cannot delegate your *responsibility*, you can delegate your *authority*. In my case, I'm required to sign a form that says my accountant has the authority to speak to the tax department on my behalf. Notice the difference: responsibility cannot be delegated, but authority can.

Let's continue to clear away this roadblock. The difference is easier understood if you associate authority with power or control. For example, the police have the power to issue a ticket to a speeding driver by virtue of the authority that has been granted to them. They have a civic duty to issue a ticket because of their responsibility

AUTHORITY IS DIRECTED DOWN- WARDS, WHEREAS RESPONSIBILITY IS DIRECTED UPWARDS.

to their superiors. Their authority relates to their relationship to the driver; their responsibility relates to their relationship to their superior. Authority is directed downwards, whereas responsibility is directed upwards. It's helpful if you use the right preposition in the right place. When using the word responsibility, follow it up by using the preposition *to*. When using the word authority, follow it up by using the preposition *over*.

Now that you're clear on how we can use the terms, you can see that while a board cannot delegate its responsibility, it can delegate its authority. So it would appear that the solution is simply to delegate all these details to someone else so that you can relax. Right?

Whoa, not so fast. In a subsequent chapter, we will look at how a board can make sure that what it has delegated is being taken care of. In the meantime, you need to get this

IF THERE'S ONE THING WORSE THAN A BOARD TRYING TO TAKE CARE OF ALL THE DETAILS ITSELF, IT'S DELEGATING EVERYTHING AND NEVER FOLLOWING UP.

delegation of authority thing clear or you'll have an even bigger train wreck. If there's one thing worse than a board trying to take care of all the details itself, it's delegating everything and never following up.

As a board that has the freedom to delegate authority, there are three things to keep in mind. The first is being absolutely clear about what the board is—and is not—delegating. It's critical that there be mutual clarity about what's being delegated. Not only must the board be clear about what is being delegated, it must also be clear to the person to whom the authority has been delegated. We'll look at this in more detail in a later chapter, but suffice to say that clarity means there's absolutely no ambiguity surrounding what has been delegated.

Having delegated with clarity, the second item of importance is knowing to whom the authority has been being delegated. There must

BOARDS ARE NOTORIOUS FOR *SORT OF* DELEGATING SOMETHING TO ITS PAS-TOR AND THEN *SORT OF* DELEGATING THE SAME THING TO A COMMITTEE.

be no ambiguity around who is—and who is not—the delegatee. Remember that church board we talked about which had a dozen committees as well as a pastor and staff? Boards are notorious for *sort of* delegating something to its pastor and then *sort of* delegating the same thing to a committee. An example is the church that has a member care committee charged with regularly visiting the church constituents but then upbraids the pastor for not connecting with the flock. This is a good reason to make sure that *what* is delegated and *to whom* it is delegated is stated unequivocally.

Sometimes a board delegates some decisions around operational expenses to someone other than the pastor. The problem with this is that such decisions interfere with the pastor's means to manage the operations. One of the principles of Policy Governance is that no subparts of the board, such as committees or officers, can be given jobs that interfere with, duplicate, or obscure the job given to the CEO.

If you hang around Policy Governance practitioners, you will be constantly confronted with the principle *of clarity and coherence of delegation*. One of the primary characteristics of Policy Governance is the absolute non-ambiguity around the issue of delegation.

Let's remind ourselves that the board has a responsibility to its owners. It and it alone is directly accountable to the owners to make sure that what should happen happens and what shouldn't happen

ONE OF THE PRIMARY CHARACTERIS-TICS OF POLICY GOVERNANCE IS THE ABSOLUTE NON-AMBIGUITY AROUND THE ISSUE OF DELEGATION.

doesn't happen. It can't shift that accountability even if it has delegated the authority. So now that your board has clearly delegated some or all of its authority and everyone is clear as to what has been delegated, to whom the authority has been granted, and what the expectations are, everything should run smoothly—ideally.

Remember the example of delegating the authority to prepare your tax return to an accountant? Come to think of it, you never heard back from her. You didn't get any emails or calls. You didn't get any forms in the mail to sign. You didn't get an invoice either, which should set off some warning bells. And it's well past the tax deadline. If you talk about your tax return to a member of a church board that has implemented a hybrid version of Policy Governance (which isn't Policy Governance at all), that person may tell you not to worry, saying that you've delegated the authority for completing your tax return to your accountant and so she's responsible. The only problem with that logic is that you're the one who will receive an unfriendly notice from the tax department.

When a board delegates authority to one person and sets the expectations, it still maintains the ultimate responsibility. That's why a church board that has implemented Policy Governance will always monitor what it has delegated to make sure its expectations are met. Later on, we will devote an entire chapter to address how a board can systematically make sure that its expectations are met. We'll look at the greatest expectation of any healthy church: making a difference in the lives of the people it's trying to reach.

10

DOES YOUR CHURCH EXIST FOR MORE THAN WHAT IT DOES?

This chapter isn't about developing a clear, concise, compelling, and creative mission statement. You won't find that in any of the other chapters in this book either. Don't misunderstand me: mission statements have their place—just not in this book. However, before we go any further, let me suggest an interesting exercise: Google "church mission statements."

Welcome back. I'm guessing you found a wide variety of mission statements. Some were cute bylines, others awkward, wordy, and cumbersome. Many were a regurgitation of the Great Commission that Jesus gave; others were some derivative of it. If you looked at ten mission statements, I would be surprised if more than one didn't have a verb. Of course, if any church is going to have a mission statement, one would assume the church is going to be *doing* something. But is the effectiveness of a church measured by what it *does?* Is it successful if it has programming for every age level? Does a resource center in part justify the existence of the church if lots of people drop by? What a tragedy if patrons of the resource center leave without getting the resources they need. Is a full sanctuary the true mark of real ministry? Suppose your church has programming,

> IS THE EFFECTIVENESS OF A CHURCH MEASURED BY WHAT IT *DOES?*

but only a few people avail themselves of what's offered. Or what if the attendance is huge, but people aren't embracing the message or growing in their faith? What if the church is deemed to be successful primarily because people are defecting from other churches? Maybe the resource center has great information, but the people receiving that information aren't doing anything with it.

John Carver introduced the concept of *ends*[13] as something a board must be able to define. Of course, ends in themselves aren't original, but the shift from the standard mission statement, visioning exercises, and strategic planning to a focus on ends is something new to many church boards. The concept of ends isn't quite the same as one might generally think of ends. The term *ends* isn't Policy Governance parlance for a church's mission or its ministry goals. You don't figure it out by deciding what the really important programs are within a church. So what are ends?

The ends of any church can be defined by answering three fundamental questions. Let's start by asking the first question in a variety of ways. How will people be better off because your church exists? What kind of changes in people's lives would you expect to see if your church is successful? What will people become as a result of being impacted by your church?

Try to answer any one of these questions without talking about what your church *does*. Arguably it really doesn't matter what your church is doing if it doesn't make a difference in someone's life. The difference shouldn't be in what the church *does* but in changed people.[14]

> ...IT REALLY DOESN'T MATTER WHAT YOUR CHURCH IS DOING IF IT DOESN'T MAKE A DIFFERENCE IN SOMEONE'S LIFE.

Does the distinguishing of ends and means seem semantical? It will seem that way if you believe that what a church *does* automatically equates to changed lives. Ends and means will appear to be a nuanced way of saying the same thing if you measure how well your church is doing by how many people attend your Sunday morning service. Keep in mind that at this point you have no idea if there is any change in the hearts and lives of the people coming to your church.

---

[13] We will use the lowercase when speaking of "ends" as a concept or idea and capitalize the term when referring to the category of Ends policies.

[14] It's ironic that a nonreligious Policy Governance system implicitly challenges the local church to a higher and more biblical standard than that to which many churches hold themselves.

Let's have a dialogue.

Q: So why does your church exist?

A: We're here to make disciples of Jesus Christ.

Q: And how is that working out?

A: Well, our church is growing. More and more people are coming to our worship services. We had a record number of people registered for our new believer's class, and many of our members are involved in home Bible studies.

Q: Are the people who attend your worship services worshipping and growing in their faith? It's wonderful to hear about the response to your new believer's class. How many actually attended the class? How many completed it? What did the attendees learn as a result of attending? Are those involved in your home Bible studies studying the Bible, and if so, what difference is that making in their lives?

Once we figure out what the difference, result, or benefit will be in people's lives, the second question we need to ask is who will be better off. What demographic is your church targeting? What geographic area is your church focusing on? Who are the intended recipients? Often churches have no idea who they're seeking to reach. I know of a church that moved out of the core area of a city because it didn't want to deal with the prostitution and crime where it had been located for over eighty years. But when I asked the leaders who they wanted to reach, they had no idea. They were only clear about who they *didn't* want to reach. The right answer to the question regarding who will be reached is not *people*, but specifically *which* people. It could be everyone in a certain geographic area or community, but no church is going to be everything for everybody.

I consulted with a church that has a university across the street and rooming houses behind it. The pastor wanted to reach the university students, while the congregation was content to populate their church with suburbanites. The people in the rooming houses didn't seem to get much consideration when it came to who the beneficiaries of the church's ministry might be.

The third question that needs to be answered in determining the ends of your church is the cost-benefit or worth. If your church decided on certain results, what other results would not be realized? If your church intends to emphasize a certain nationality or socioeconomic group, how does that impact those who it may not otherwise reach? In fairness to the church that relocated from an area of the city which had the criminal element, it considered cost. It realized that if it poured its resources into reaching that demographic, in all likelihood it would preclude others from attending the church. The cost-benefit or worth considers the overall result, including the priority of certain benefits for certain people. It also considers efficiency. For example, if the results for the recipients can be achieved at a certain cost and it is actually costing more than that amount, is it worth it?

So once you've answered the *what, for whom,* and *worth* questions, you're there. Identify the intended results, the intended recipients, and the cost-benefit or worth and you have your ends. Sounds easy? Try it again. Answer the ends question without mentioning anything that your church *does*. See if your ends statement refers to *what the intended recipients will be* or *what they will have* rather than *what your church will do* or *what it will provide*.

> CHURCHES ARE ADDICTED TO ACTIVITY. FAITHFULNESS TRUMPS FRUITFULNESS. SUCCESS IS A SWEAR WORD. BUSYNESS SHIELDS A CHURCH FROM ASKING IF IT'S MAKING ANY DIFFERENCE.

So why is it so hard to state ends in the context of Policy Governance? Because churches are addicted to activity. Faithfulness trumps fruitfulness. Success is a swear word. Busyness shields a church from asking if it's making any difference. If your church could state its ends without describing what it's going to do (and the Policy Governance system would insist that it must), how would you know that your ends were being accomplished? You want people to be more biblically informed, but how do you know that result is being achieved? "Our pastor is a great Bible teacher" doesn't answer the question. That's just a subjective comment on how he or she sounds. One of your ends might be that people who attend your church will be passionate disciples of Jesus Christ. "Our church is growing" means that your services are popular, and it may even imply that people are passionate, but are they becoming more passionate followers of Christ?

It's impossible for you to want something without having a way to know if what you want is obtained. To want something (or to want more of what you already have) implies that either you don't currently have it or don't have enough of it. You can't have a purpose without knowing if that purpose can or cannot be achieved. There's no such thing as having a desire without knowing if that desire can or cannot be fulfilled. Consider anything you might want in life. Anything! If you want a fulfilling marriage, you'll be able to describe characteristics that indicate you have—or don't have—a fulfilling marriage. Your desire for your children is that they be successful in life. To have that desire assumes you have some idea what success for your kids would look like. Then you'll be able to determine if your desire has been satisfied.

> IT'S IMPOSSIBLE FOR YOU TO WANT SOMETHING WITHOUT HAVING A WAY TO KNOW IF WHAT YOU WANT IS OBTAINED.

The church is no different. Ends *can* be measured—and they *must* be measured. If one of the ends includes your people developing into mature Christ followers, somehow there must be a way of knowing whether they have attained some level of maturity. If your church wants to see people's lives changed, it must know what that would look like and if the intended changes have taken place.

Sadly, many churches take the easy way out. Instead of articulating ends which are aligned with God's intention for people, they stop at programs and functions which can be measured by activity. Seeing the right changes in others is often viewed as the same as the church doing the right things. Your church only has great ministries if the result of those ministries is changed lives.

> SADLY, MANY CHURCHES TAKE THE EASY WAY OUT. INSTEAD OF ARTICULATING ENDS WHICH ARE ALIGNED WITH GOD'S INTENTION FOR PEOPLE, THEY STOP AT PROGRAMS AND FUNCTIONS WHICH CAN BE MEASURED BY ACTIVITY.

We don't operate this way in other areas of our lives. We exercise to lose weight. But if we never weigh ourselves, how do we know if the exercise is producing the intended results?

Would we make investments to increase our financial position, but never check the value of our portfolio? So why would we think of doing it in the context of something we allege has eternal implications? That view is not only unbiblical, it will drive your church to complete apathy—or total insanity. Think about it. Why would your church exist to see something accomplished yet have no idea if it is being accomplished—that is, unless programming and busyness equates to accomplishment?

So what about the missionary in Africa who preaches the gospel for twenty-five years and sees no converts? Good question. But they weren't there just to preach. They must have had some way of finding out if their message was being heard, even if no one was responding to it. It wouldn't have made sense for the missionary to preach for twenty-five years in a language that wasn't understood. So they would at least have to know if their message was being comprehended.

WHY WOULD YOUR CHURCH EXIST TO SEE SOMETHING ACCOMPLISHED YET HAVE NO IDEA IF IT IS BEING ACCOMPLISHED—THAT IS, UNLESS PROGRAMMING AND BUSYNESS EQUATES TO ACCOMPLISHMENT?

The concept of ends challenges a board to ask what results the church wants to see. Will the owners of the church be satisfied to have a variety of well-attended programs? Will the efforts of the church be judged as worthwhile if pews are filled on Sunday mornings? Has it arrived when the mortgage-burning ceremony takes place? Or is there something more?

Success in the church must be defined by what *the intended beneficiaries will become*, not by what the church *will do*.

11

WHAT'S THE DIFFERENCE BETWEEN AN OWNER AND A CONSUMER?

My son-in-law Tom is part-owner of a chain of shoe stores. Often when he's with a supplier, he will text my daughter with a picture of a shoe along with the message, "What do you think?" Marcie will reply, "For me or for the stores?" Let's figure out how Tom answers that question.

In the previous chapter, we learned about the Policy Governance principle of ends. The ends of a church are defined when it has identified the intended benefits in the lives of the intended beneficiaries along with the cost-benefit or worth of the change in the lives of those people. Before that, we looked at the Policy Governance principle of ownership and the need to decide which people own the ministry of the church. We've also looked at board members who comprise a board that governs on behalf of the owners. We haven't looked at the role of management yet, but we'll address that in some depth later in the book.

There are four groups of people who make up your church: the owners, the board, the staff (including volunteers), and finally the beneficiaries or recipients of your ministry. Now this is where things start to get complicated.

But first let's go back to my son-in-law and the question my daughter posed. For Tom to answer the question, he needs to understand it. For Marcie to answer, she needs to understand his question. So is Tom asking the question of his wife as a potential customer? Is he asking if Marcie would like a pair of shoes like the ones in the picture? If so, he's asking a *beneficiary* or *consumer* question. Does she like the shoes?

What's her personal preference? However, if he's asking a question of his wife, who is also an owner, then he's asking an *owner* question. He wants her opinion regarding whether she thinks enough people will like the style of the shoe to justify the space it will take on the display table or the room that the inventory will occupy in the warehouse. Her answer depends on what role she is occupying.[15]

You can see how it's impossible to slot everyone in the church exclusively into one of the four groups. There will be people who are part of all four groups. Because you are reading this book, you may be one of those people. You may be on the board, which in all likelihood means you are also one of the owners. If you volunteer as a youth sponsor, usher at a service, or lead a home Bible study, you're a volunteer, which makes you part of a group that does the ministry. As someone who regularly attends the services and benefits from the church, you're one of the beneficiaries.

Back again to Tom's question. It's imperative, critical, mandatory— whatever adjective you want to use—that Marcie is unambiguously clear about what group she's in when she answers the question. Failure to do so can have a very negative impact. If she answers a consumer question with an owner answer, she could end up with a pair of shoes she doesn't like. A more costly error will result if she answers an owner question with a consumer answer. The organization could end up with shoes that are preferred by only her and a select few.

Policy Governance is about clarity of roles and non-ambiguity. Clarity and non-ambiguity results in part from making sure that in any conversation, you are clear regarding the hat—or shoe—you're wearing and the group you're talking about.

I have four different sports jerseys and shirts.[16] Which jersey I wear depends on which sporting event I'm going to. If I'm going to a NASCAR race, I won't wear my Packers jersey. If I'm going to a Winnipeg Jets

---

[15] This analogy is intended to distinguish between owners and consumers. I'm not suggesting that moral owners in a church context should become involved in the details of how the ends are achieved.

[16] Actually, the number is a little greater than that, but I'll make it four for the purpose of this illustration.

hockey game, I won't wear a NASCAR t-shirt. I guess I can wear all four at the same time, but only one will be visible. Deciding which jersey I'll wear is easy once I've decided where I'm going.

Every time you look at a church issue, you must decide what jersey you're wearing. In too many situations, owners wear their beneficiary or consumer jerseys. It might be twenty-below at Lambeau Field, but they'll still sport their NASCAR t-shirts. When that happens, complaints will sometimes sound like this: "I'm a member (an owner) of this church and as such I'd like to talk to a board member about how much I hate the music." Notice the contradiction. If this person was a genuine owner concerned about whether the music was an effective means of connecting with the intended beneficiaries, then his or her personal preference in music would be inconsequential.[17] If my daughter responds to her husband's text from the perspective of an owner, her personal preference about the shoes will be irrelevant. She'll only be concerned about whether enough consumers will want that type of shoe.

Making the distinction between an owner and a beneficiary is a challenge for your church board. Even though the board may have grasped the Policy Governance principle of a board being the voice and agent of its owners, it's easy to lose focus. The board should be listening to the owners to understand what difference the owners want to make in the lives of an identifiable group of people.

If you have sat on the board of a church for more than half an hour, you will recognize that a good portion of the board's four-hour Monday evening meeting is taken up with responding to the concerns of those who perceive themselves as owners but talk and act like consumers. (The rest of the time is spent delving into the details of management, but that's a topic for a future chapter.) We've heard the complaint that churches have a consumer mentality.

> WHEN WE TREAT OWNERS LIKE CONSUMERS, THEY WILL RESPOND AS CONSUMERS.

---

[17] This does not mean that owners should weigh in on the means of achieving the ends of their church, including means which are unacceptable. This example is only intended to highlight the idea that true owners care about the advancement of the ends of the church, not their personal preferences.

49

When we treat owners like consumers, they will respond as consumers. Add in frustrated pastors who leave the church beaten up and burnt out because they don't know who they're preaching to. Are they addressing the intended beneficiaries in whose lives the owners allege they're longing to see change, or are they directing their comments at a bunch of self-confessed and self-indulgent owners who are prepared to fire the pastor if their consumeristic appetite

> THE CHURCH WANTS THE CONSUMER TO BE SO ENAMORED WITH THE CHANGE THAT THE PRODUCT HAS MADE IN THEIR LIVES THAT THEY WANT TO BECOME A SHAREHOLDER.

isn't satiated? When looking at an issue or listening to a question, you must decide if you're viewing it as an owner or a consumer.

Evangelical churches profess to exist to make owners out of beneficiaries. Using the analogy of a for-profit corporation, the church wants the consumer to be so enamored with the change that the product has made in their lives that they want to become a shareholder.

If the pastor of your church is familiar and comfortable with Policy Governance, it allows him or her to address beneficiaries with a view to having those consumers becoming owners.

If the moral owners in your church have an understanding and appreciation of their role as owners, they will surrender their personal preferences to the greater cause of the church. They'll be less occupied with their comfort and convenience and become far more concerned that the ministries of the church have the desired impact on the people in whose lives they as owners long to see change.

12

BUT SHOULDN'T THE CHURCH BE DOING SOMETHING?

A group of us stood around the water cooler, debriefing about the weekend. One of our colleagues was a particularly proud dad.

"Austin's football team played a great game," he said. "They had over three hundred yards passing, another 157 yards rushing, won the time of possession, and didn't turn the ball over once."

"So what was the final score?" I interjected, more because I needed to get back to work and less because I was interested in his stats report.

"Hmm… good question."

"Who won?"

He shrugged as though my question was inconsequential. "I didn't bother to check."

Bizarre? Not really. Churches do it all the time.

We've looked at why a particular local church exists. The Policy Governance principle of ends has now led us away from focusing on what the church is doing and toward what people are becoming. Maybe, as you've read along, you've been muttering to yourself, "But how are these people supposed to change if we don't tell them anything? How will they learn anything if we don't teach them? How are they going to be beneficiaries if we don't provide some kind of benefit?" These questions are as wise as asking how a football team plans to win a game if it doesn't implement its playbook by completing passes, rushing the ball, avoiding turnovers, and playing solid defense. Of course all that needs to happen. But that's not why a team plays football. It plays to win.

What you're asking about is something referred to in Policy Governance as *means*. If you have the concept of ends locked down, then understanding means will be easy. Means refer to anything that's not an end. Everything your church does is a means to accomplishing the ends for which it exists. This includes such things as cutting the grass, maintaining the parking lot, and managing the church kitchen.

> MEANS REFER TO ANYTHING THAT'S NOT AN END. EVERYTHING YOUR CHURCH DOES IS A MEANS TO ACCOMPLISHING THE ENDS FOR WHICH IT EXISTS.

"But surely everything a church does is not a means," you say. Your thoughts may have just raced to the worship service on Sunday morning. It's far and away the biggest thing you do at your church. If a church doesn't have a worship service, it would hardly qualify as a church, so surely that shouldn't be reduced to a means.

Let's see if you have a point. So your church exists—at least in part—to have worship services. *Why* does it have worship services? Is it merely for the sake of the services themselves? What if your church conducted weekly worship services characterized by quality music and powerful sermons but people didn't respond with God-focused worship and life-altering decisions? Should it be assumed that if the music is of sufficient quality and the sermons are powerful enough, people will experience the kind of change in their lives that the owners are looking for? You can assume there'll be change, but assuming isn't the same as knowing. To know for sure, you would need to make some kind of qualitative determination that quality music and powerful sermons *in themselves* change lives. But that's impossible under your first assumption. If you don't believe it's possible to know for sure that lives have been changed, then ipso facto it is impossible to know if lives have been changed through quality music and powerful sermons.

You can't have an end that people's lives will be changed if you can't delineate what kind of change you want to see. Suppose, for example, a changed life would include a person becoming a "mature believer." What does that look like? Remember that you can't desire something that cannot potentially be obtained. As such, you can't desire to see spiritual maturity in the lives of your constituents if there's no possible way of knowing that spiritual maturity has taken place.

You might argue that surveys have been done in your church to find out if people enjoy the services and the results have been consistently positive; therefore, your ends are being accomplished. However, your ends likely don't include something like "Because ABC Church exists, people will enjoy church services." If your ends sound like that, then just by having enough people who previously didn't enjoy church services now enjoying them would indicate an accomplishment of ends. However, it still doesn't address why it's important just to have people enjoy church services.

But don't we believe that ultimately only God can produce change in people's lives independently of us? If that's true, we don't have to concern ourselves with ends which we can neither accomplish nor measure. Based on that assumption, it follows that we don't need to bother with any of the means that might be necessary to accomplish the ends. That argument would imply that the church should only concern itself with *doing church*. In that case, it doesn't matter if there is quality music and powerful messages, because those things don't lead to the change we would want but could never confirm.

Means either don't matter or they do. If they don't matter, then a church can do whatever it wants to do however it wants to do it, because what it does isn't important. If means do matter, then there must be a way of knowing what difference those means are making.

> HOW DOES THE CHURCH KNOW IF WHAT IT'S DOING IS EFFECTIVE AND WORTHWHILE IF IT NEVER LOOKS AT THE END RESULTS?

On the one hand, it isn't the church's job to make changes in people's lives. On the other hand, the church has a responsibility to provide the very best environment and education so that the change it wants to see can take place.

How does the church know if what it's doing is effective and worthwhile if it never looks at the end results? Means are as important as ends, to the extent that they facilitate the accomplishment of ends. However, the problem with many (most) churches is that the means *become* the ends.

So how do you keep the idea of ends and means separate? The easiest way is to go back to your definitions of ends. If you're describing the ultimate benefit for the intended beneficiaries and the cost-benefit associated with it, you're talking about ends. If you aren't describing ends, then you're talking about means. Worship services, Bible studies, tithing, and evangelism are all means. They are the passes, rushes, and tackles that a church needs to perform if it's going to be successful in winning the game.

Let me encourage your board to always ask the question *why*: "Why is our church doing what it's doing?" It needs to keep asking why until it lands on an answer that describes the changes it wants to see in the lives of people. Make sure as well that it's an answer that justifies the resources invested in seeing those changes.

What is the role of the board in all this?

The role of the board is to define the ends as they reflect the intentions of those who own the ministry of the church, and then ensure that the ends are accomplished. This brings us to a landmark we have seen before: delegation. It's here that the board will clearly and unambiguously delegate authority for the accomplishment of the ends to one person. Policy Governance refers to the role of that person as the chief executive officer, the one person the board authorizes to use any means (almost) to accomplish the ends. In our next chapter, we will see how that can be done.

13

DO ANY MEANS
JUSTIFY THE ENDS?

We discovered in our last chapter that anything that's not an end is a means. Ends and means are mutually exclusive. It's not that ends are important and means are just details. However noble the ends of any church might be, they will not be accomplished without the church doing something. The Apostle Paul reminded the first-century church in Corinth that the change which needed to take place in people's lives could only be done by God. However, He has chosen to put His treasure into humans, who are described as clay pots.

In the introduction, I mentioned that the title of pastor is often used to describe the individual who occupies the CEO role and provides executive leadership to a church. The term pastor is often preceded with the adjective *lead* or *senior*. Sometimes the chief executive role is filled by an executive pastor who may not have an upfront or pulpit role but provides overall administrative leadership. Keep in mind that the focus of this chapter isn't on the title or the term. Most churches have someone who they identify as the leader, so for the sake of consistency I will refer to the person fulfilling the CEO role as the pastor.

Let's remember that Policy Governance is vastly different

> ONCE THE BOARD HAS DEFINED THE ENDS, IT FREES UP THE PASTOR TO USE ANY MEANS TO ACCOMPLISH THE ENDS, EXCEPT THOSE WHICH THE BOARD EXPLICITLY PROHIBITS

than the typical governance model used by most churches. With that in mind, brace yourself to be shocked by the implications of the next statement: once the board has defined the ends, it frees up the pastor to use any means to accomplish the ends, except those which the board explicitly prohibits.

As I spend time with church leaders and boards, one of the greatest challenges—likely the greatest challenge—is reconciling the role of the board with the role of the pastor. Like the old days, when there were smoking and non-smoking sections in restaurants, the smoke of administration often wafts between the pastor's office and the board room. No one is quite sure where one section ends and the next one starts. Sometimes the pastor is the chair of the board. Sometimes he or she sits on the board, along with some of the staff. In other situations, the pastor is an ex officio member of the board.[18] There are situations, more so in smaller churches, where the pastor is the administrative assistant to the board and preaches as often as the board chooses—and sometimes even on topics of the board's choosing.

One of the greatest temptations for a board which has decided to implement Policy Governance is to become involved in telling the pastor how to accomplish the ends. One reason is that it's been a habit. Boards traditionally have become unwittingly addicted to controlling the means used to accomplish the ends. Trying to break this habit leaves most boards in a cold sweat, fidgeting uncontrollably and biting their collective tongues. But they must not give in. One sniff will have them falling off the Policy Governance wagon and run over by the wheels of conventionalism. This let's-weigh-in-on-non-prohibited-means drug is so dangerous that it shouldn't even be allowed inside the board room.

A board that uses Policy Governance understands that it cannot be directive when it comes to means. It knows it can't have a drink, but it sometimes leaves the bottle on the board table. This sometimes poses as "Pastor, do you mind if I make a suggestion?" The bottle gets a little closer to the glass when a board member says, "Don't feel any obligation, but I wonder if you've thought of…" When this happens, the Policy Governance principle about clarity gets smudged. The pastor won't be clear whether it's a suggestion or a veiled directive.

---

[18] Practically, ex officio means that the person is sort of on the board and sort of not. See the reference to smoking and non-smoking sections above.

But what if the pastor does something the board doesn't like? What if the service times are changed or an executive pastor is hired without vetting the candidate through the board? What if the worship style is changed? You know, the big stuff. If changes are being made with which your board is uncomfortable, the board needs to ask itself what value is being compromised by these changes. Maybe it hasn't defined its ends with sufficient focus and clarity. However, in most cases it will be a matter of preference. If that's the case, I refer your board back to the chapter on owners and consumers.

In fairness to the board, there are going to be means that a pastor could use that a board could—and possibly should—find unacceptable. A Policy Governance board will deal with these in a document called Executive Limitation[19] policies. These policies are always stated in a non-directive and proscriptive way, using language such as "shall not cause" or "shall not allow." You won't listen to the critics of Policy Governance for very long before you come across objections to the use of negative language. The argument you might hear is that negative and prohibitive language is demotivating and pushes the CEO to be risk-averse.

In many traditional boards, any means are deemed unacceptable unless they are approved by the board. Boards using Policy Governance, on the other hand, have preapproved the pastor's use of *any* means except ones the board has specifically prohibited. Using this system releases the pastor from going to the board for approval regarding decisions about which the board might arbitrarily want to have input. It also liberates the pastor from the constant fear that his or her wrists will be slapped for something the board decides it doesn't like. Prohibited means are based on a board's values, not on the personal distaste of any or all board members. Keep asking the question *why*. As the board considers limiting the means a pastor can use, asking why forces the board to consider the value which underlies its limitation.

Let's illustrate this idea using a non-church example with which you may be all too familiar. If you're the parent of a child sixteen years of age

---

[19] We will use the lowercase when referring to the concept of executive limitations. When referring to Executive Limitation policies, we will capitalize the term.

or older, you will have been faced with the question, "Can I borrow the car?" What's your first response? If it's no, the follow-up question will be "Why?" Your newbie driver is trying to drill down to discover the underlying value behind your denial. "Cuz it's my car" will likely suffice at home, but it's less likely to deepen the trust relationship between a board and its pastor.

If your teen's request is worthy of consideration, you might ask something like, "Where are you going?" This approach creates problems for both you and your child. First, you only have a vague idea what an acceptable answer might be, and second, your driver only has a vague idea what would constitute an acceptable destination. Suppose they respond by saying that they're going to a friend's house. You're likely to follow up by asking which friend they're going to see. Eventually you may reluctantly concede to their request with an elusive sense of dis-ease, followed up by admonitions to drive safely and return on time, which are only heard by the inside of the door.

The problem is that you're reacting to their request rather than proactively limiting their use of the car based on your values. The iron-ic part is that you have values that you could articulate to yourself—and to your teen—if only you had dug deep enough to consider them. These values could be expressed as limitations because your concern is likely less about where you want them to go and more about where you *don't* want them to go. Who you would like them to see is less sig-nificant than who you *don't* want them to see. Because they have their license, you don't need to tell them how to drive the car. However, you may want to attach some limitations as to how they are *not* to drive the car.

Here are some limitations that may reflect your values:

1. They cannot use the car if either you or your spouse needs it.
2. They cannot break any laws.
3. They cannot drive the car to meet with persons of ill repute.
4. They cannot use the car between the hours of midnight and 6:00 a.m.

Notice that you have not been directive. You haven't told them anything about where they should go or who they can see or what routes to take. You have defined your values and then limited their driving activities as a reflection of those values. In doing this, you have satisfied your concerns by proactively limiting actions which would compromise your values.

In a subsequent chapter, we'll look at the importance of monitoring compliance to limitations. For now it's important to understanding the Policy Governance principle of Executive Limitations. In developing executive limitations, your board needs to reflect on its values around any illegal, unethical, or imprudent means which, if used by your pastor, would violate those values.

The principle of Executive Limitation policies can be very freeing for your board. These policies allow your board to think through its values as they relate to those means that would be unacceptable in accomplishing the ends of the church, even if they worked. The values that make certain means unacceptable will be communicated to your pastor by clearly stating them in the form of boundary-setting policies.

Executive limitations aren't just about developing and writing policies. They're about identifying the values of your church board and ensuring those values aren't compromised.

But how does a board make sure every value is covered? While that may sound ominous, it's less overwhelming than you might first think.

14

How Can a Board Limit
the Size of Its Policy Manual?

You've seen this movie before. A policy manual is mind-numbingly compiled and then meticulously bound. The policy committee celebrates the completion of a job it never wanted to do in the first place. Then the manual is placed on the top shelf where no one can reach it—assuming anyone would want to. It's only dragged down when it serves the purpose of some precisionist. Your Policy Governance manual won't look like that. It will be a document that passionately and practically reflects the values of your board. It will be comprised of four sets of policies. We have referred to Ends policies, and in this chapter we will look at Executive Limitation policies. Later on you will be introduced to Governance Process policies and Board-Management Delegation policies.

Every set of policies will be developed using the Policy Governance principle of policy sizes. For now let's look at how this relates to Executive Limitation policies.

John Carver refers to the idea of policy sizes as a series of nesting bowls, each bowl contained within a larger bowl. The largest bowl symbolizes the broadest policy. In the same way that the largest nesting bowl holds all the other bowls, so the broadest policy envelops every policy within it.

Each of the four sections of your board policy manual (these include Ends policies, Executive Limitation policies, Governance Process policies, and Board-Management Delegation policies) will begin with a very broad statement which can be referred to as the global policy. In the Executive Limitations section, this policy might state that "the pastor shall not cause or allow any practice, activity, decision, or organizational circumstance which is unbiblical, unlawful, imprudent, unethical, or violates the church's statement of faith." A board may change or add to this wording. For example, some boards expand this global level statement to prohibit "any violation of generally accepted professional or business principles."

After I've introduced Policy Governance to a church board and it has decided to begin the process of implementing the system, the next step is to meet for the purpose of drafting policies. I never go in with a blank sheet. That would be a waste of time and drive everyone crazy. Besides, many churches, never mind thousands of organizations, have done this before, so there are some boilerplate policies to get the board started. As such, I start with the global policy and then suggest the board members break up into groups of three or four to see if they can uncover any board value that wouldn't be covered by this policy.

But before they shuffle their chairs—and waste their time—we discover together that the global policy covers every concern a board could have in relation to the means used by the pastor to advance the ends of the church. As long as the pastor doesn't do anything that's unbiblical, unlawful, imprudent (as in unwise or just plain dumb), unethical, or violates the church's statement of faith, he or she can use any means to accomplish the ends. The problem with using just a global policy is that it's complete but not comprehensive. It is analogous to telling your teen driver not to do anything imprudent, then reprimanding them when they come home fifteen minutes after eleven on a school night. You might say, "I told you not to do anything imprudent, and coming home at 11:15 was imprudent." Your instructions were complete but not comprehensive. You knew that having your child get a good night's sleep was a value and not doing so would be imprudent. However, your child might attempt to justify, by pointing out the bedtime of their peers, that 11:15 *is* a prudent time to come home. The problem is that you didn't reflect that value clearly enough in your policy.

As it relates to the role of your board and the pastor, maybe this nesting policy idea doesn't make sense to you. After all, why wouldn't you just list all the specific limitations in the first place and be done with

TED HULL

the broader limitations, including that global policy? The global policy is so general and vague that it seems virtually meaningless.

That's an interesting idea, so let's start by leaving out the global policy and get right to the bottom line. Let's develop a policy for *every* means that would be unacceptable to your board, keeping in mind that anything the board does not limit is acceptable. Now your board will have a list of detailed limitations. There may be ten executive limitations or a hundred. What you'll have is a hundred small bowls covering the limitation table. The challenge will be those means which fall between the bowls. Regardless of how many policies your board has, they won't state its core values. The global policy limits every means that is unbiblical, unlawful, imprudent, unethical, or violates the church's statement of faith. Every other limitation fits within the global bowl in order of increasing specificity.

We're used to legal documents that intentionally protect the one who develops the contract. They can be filled with fine print or intentional ambiguity which is intended to protect the writer of the contract. Executive limitations should never be written that way. They are not intended to cover the board or trap the pastor. They need to be very carefully worded with a view to clarity, allowing the pastor to reasonably interpret the policy.

The principle of policy sizes is critical in the effective use of Policy Governance. A broad, inclusive policy isn't enough. Executive limitations aren't intended to be breadcrumbs that your board drops along the path, all the while hoping your pastor figures out what the board wants. Nor should your executive limitations be a litany of detailed policies that leaves out the core values of the board.

When your teen takes your car, he or she shouldn't be wondering what you value. They don't want to get home only to find out that you have an additional limitation you didn't tell them about. The limitations must be clear. Every limitation should reflect your broadest values: no bad driving, bad company, bad marks, or bad moods (one of the results of not getting enough sleep).

The same principle applies to the limitations your board places on your pastor. Executive limitations should be clear, not ambiguous, *pro*scriptive rather than *pre*scriptive. They should place limits rather than provide direction. Once the board has established and defined its values, it will allow the pastor to reasonably interpret the policies.

15

WHY DOES THE PASTOR
GET TO INTERPRET THE POLICIES?

In the last chapter, we looked at policy sizes. We started with the global policy that limited your pastor from using a means which was unbiblical, unlawful, imprudent, unethical, or violated the church's statement of faith. The global policy is analogous to the largest nesting bowl we referred to in the previous chapter. It's the umbrella which covers all executive limitations. Then we saw that the board could go into more detail until it was willing to accept any reasonable interpretation. So how does this "any reasonable interpretation" principle work?

Let's go back to the example of your young driver. Remember that one of your limitations included him or her from meeting people of ill repute? If you served on a typical board and you transposed those principles to dealing with your teen, you would insist that every person your child met must be prescreened. If that wasn't possible, you would assess them after the fact. You would interpret what "ill repute" meant, arbitrarily deciding what that meant to you. The Policy Governance principle of "any reasonable interpretation" doesn't work like that. It would allow your teen to interpret what you meant, as long as an average person would agree that the interpretation was reasonable.

But if the board has made the policy, shouldn't it have the right to interpret it? No! If you want to say something you haven't said, then say it. If you haven't said it, it means that any reasonable interpretation of the broader policy is sufficient. Let's look again at our analogy. It would be difficult to reasonably argue that someone who has three outstanding drug charges isn't a person of ill repute. What about the fact that the girl with whom your son spent some time has a reputation for missing three-point shots on her high school basketball team? Is that the same thing? I hope you're rolling your eyes by now. That's hardly a reasonable interpretation of your ill repute limitation.

Getting back to Policy Governance, there are three important things to keep in mind in understanding the reasonable interpretation principle. First, it's the board that develops the Executive Limitation policies. Second, it's the pastor who interprets the policy. Third, it's the board that decides if the interpretation is reasonable.

Now that we have the concept of executive limitations figured out, let's see if we can clearly understand the idea of reasonable interpretation. Maybe at this point it's sounding a little nebulous and slippery. In the Policy Governance system, interpreting is not the same as synonymizing. Can the pastor interpret the policy to mean anything that suits his or her preference? No. The board will assess the interpretation as being reasonable by using the "reasonable person" test. You don't need to be a parent of a teenager to discern the difference between hanging out with drug dealers versus spending time with lousy three-point shooters. One of those two groups would consist of people any parent wouldn't want their kid associating with. When it comes to any reasonable interpretation, it doesn't mean the interpretation of one or more of the board members. Instead the question is whether any reasonable person would see the interpretation as reasonable.

It's often necessary for the CEO to provide a benchmark for reasonableness. Imagine that my wife is packing her suitcase in preparation for an upcoming flight we're taking to an exotic resort. After packing, she asks me if her suitcase is too heavy. Because I am an expert governance consultant and understand the idea of any reasonable interpretation, I bark, "Of course it's too heavy. You've packed enough to keep half the resort clothed for a week!" She goes on to explain that she only has one change of clothes for each day and that it's unreasonable to expect she can leave some of them at home. You can readily see that using me as a reasonable person criterion isn't going to work. However, that still doesn't mean her suitcase isn't too heavy. "Heavy" can be objectively determined. When it comes to the weight of a suitcase, heavy will be greater than fifty pounds. The scale at the airport becomes the final arbiter of reasonableness. This idea is referred to as an operational definition. In this case, heavy can be objectively defined so that it means the same thing every time.

Interpreting *heavy* as far as the suitcase is concerned is relatively easy, but what about more complex issues associated with your church? Would your board have a value around the safety of children and vulnerable persons? What about the security of the church's database or the morale of its staff? What would such values translate into? You likely want executive limitations which prevent your pastor from functioning outside the scope of volunteer safety, informational security, and staff engagement. It doesn't cut it for the pastor to state that he or she is a reasonable person and doesn't let dangerous people work in the nursery, or that the church administrator copies the church's data to a thumb drive and leaves it in the ashtray of his or her car, or deciding that the staff are doing fine because the pastor insists on high morale.

Your pastor might interpret safety as it relates to children as ensuring volunteers take a certified course by a nationally recognized organization that deals with issues regarding the protection of children and vulnerable persons. One objective measurement is whether your church's insurance company will provide coverage based on the policies and procedures in place. When it comes to the integrity of church member information, there are industry-accepted standards of information security. Formally qualified human resource consultants can evaluate the level of staff morale.

A reasonable interpretation doesn't confirm that children and vulnerable persons are safe or that the database can't be hacked or that staff morale is at an appropriate level. All that's been done so far is the pastor stating what conditions he or she believes need to be in place for the board to acknowledge compliance to its limitations.

Sometimes the standard for a reasonable interpretation or operational definition is developed internally by the pastor. I worked with a church whose ends included constituents being relationally connected to the church. Based on the pastor's interpretations, it measured that by tracking whether an individual constituent had attended any function of the church (other than the Sunday worship service, which couldn't be practically tracked) or served in a volunteer capacity within the last six weeks. A benchmark for a reasonable interpretation of "relationally connected" was established as a percentage of the total constituents. The pastor and the board understood that not everyone will connect in a large church, so the pastor sets a percentage level to demonstrate the accomplishment of that particular end. Another way of identifying reasonableness is to find out what the standard is within your denomination or have a third party conduct a formal survey and share the results.

A common question revolves around the issue of the pastor's interpretation and what happens if it's not considered a reasonable interpretation by the board. To answer that, let's start with stating the reasons why an interpretation might not be reasonable.

The least common reason is that the interpretation is simply not reasonable. In other words, there is no way any reasonable person would have interpreted the policy in the way it was interpreted by the pastor. We have already looked at some "What was the pastor thinking?" examples. By the time you get to this point, the board's problem with its pastor is probably greater than unreasonable interpretations.

It often happens, especially in the early stages of policy interpretation, that a policy is reasonably interpreted as written, but the board didn't anticipate some of the implications of the policy. The policy may not have been as detailed as it should have been, or perhaps it was just poorly worded. When I consult with a board, I like to have the CEO present; he or she can often point out some potential gaps between the values of the board and how those values are reflected in the Executive Limitation policy. However, in the event that the pastor reasonably interprets the policy but misses the underlying value of the board, the board needs to reword the policy to make the limitation more explicit. A subsequent interpretation should be enough to address the board's concern.

This problem should not be confused with an interpretation that doesn't suit the preference of the board or individual board members. The board should never write a policy hoping that the pastor "gets the hint." Executive limitations are not a game of governance charades. They reflect values, not preferences.

Often an interpretation is not acceptable to the board because it's either incomplete or doesn't directly address the policy. Suppose, for example, your board has a carefully crafted policy that prohibits the pastor from allowing the church's capital assets to be unnecessarily exposed to risk, damage, or loss. The pastor needs to interpret all three terms. Interpreting exposure to risk as an inadequate or inoperable fire sprinkler or security system may partially interpret risk. However, stopping there doesn't provide an interpretation of damage or loss. At other times, an interpretation may not address the policy at all.

Another inadequate interpretation is one that's not tied to an operational definition. The interpretation of the pastor may sound reasonable to the board, but both parties may just be guessing. In the case of that heavy—or not so heavy—suitcase, Lorna and I may just be guessing. Until it's weighed, it's only a guess. In many cases, whether an interpretation is reasonable can be established by an outside authority. An example of this is an executive limitation which prohibits children from being exposed to potentially dangerous church employees or volunteers. It should be an unreasonable interpretation, and therefore unacceptable, for the pastor to simply state that the church has a policy and a handbook. There are usually independent standards in place which decide if the policy and the plan for implementation are acceptable.

A common executive limitation addresses the board's value of a working environment where employees are clear about what their job is and where the staff is treated with dignity. So let's look as an example of one policy and what that might look like in the context of a monitoring report.

Policy: With respect to the treatment of staff, the pastor may not cause or allow conditions which are unclear.[20]
Interpretation: Unclear conditions include staff not knowing:
• to whom they report.
• where office rules and policies are located.

---

[20] This policy typically limits conditions which are unsafe and undignified as well. However for the purposes of this example we will look only at the interpretation of "unclear."

- the expected output of their jobs.
- the limitations on the authority of their positions.

Compliance to this policy requires that not less than eighty percent of staff experience working conditions which are clear according to the above interpretation. This percentage was recommended by ABC Human Resource Consultants.[21] These interpretations of "unclear" were derived from consultations with ABC as well as input from church staff.

Data: I engaged the services of ABC Human Resource Consultants to interview a random sample of the staff to determine if conditions were clear. The attached report shows that 85.7 percent experienced conditions which were clear.

Therefore I report compliance.

Note that the board didn't interpret the word "clear." Nor did the pastor interpret "clear" to mean *not vague* or *unambiguous*. The interpretation included a description of what conditions would prevail which would create an unacceptable environment for the board. The interpretation included an operational definition provided by an outside source as well as staff input. The eighty-percent level acknowledges that regardless of how much effort management puts toward providing clarity, one employee in five won't get it.

We now have executive limitations which reflect the values of the board. These proscriptive policies limit the means which the pastor can use in seeing the ends of the church accomplished, even if they work. These need to be developed with sufficient detail so that the board is willing to accept any reasonable interpretation.

---

[21] A fictitious company.

16

How Does the Board Handle the Budget?

By now you can clearly distinguish between ends and means. Once you've determined the ultimate benefits that result from the existence of your local church, who the intended recipients of those benefits are, and the cost-benefit of the results, you have your ends. Everything else is a means used to accomplish the ends. The pastor is free to use *any* means except those the board has prohibited.

A BUDGET IS THE MOST OVERWORKED, OVERUSED, MISUNDERSTOOD, AND INACCURATE PIECE OF FICTION THAT A CHURCH BOARD WILL EVER SEE.

Except the budget? The board must surely be involved with that means, right? After all, if the board isn't involved in reviewing and approving the budget, how could it say with a clear conscience that it's carried out its fiduciary responsibility?

A budget is the most overworked, overused, misunderstood, and inaccurate piece of fiction that a church board will ever see. It's like a bad steak which is chewed, gnawed, and eventually choked down. Swallowing it consumes far more energy than the nutritional value it provides. I have never met a board member in my life who understood a traditional organizational budget. Boards virtually never understand what they are approving, and what they approve is never, ever complied with.

This subject consumes the most time and creates the most tension at the board table. It starts with a document itemizing the income and expenses for the upcoming fiscal year. These include individual line items detailing specific costs such as salaries, office supplies, electricity, and janitorial products. The budget goes to the board for review and approval.

It's important to keep in mind that the board approves the entire document, including every line item. For example, if the line item for electricity is $12,000, then the board is approving the expenditure of $12,000. The pastor cannot expend any more or any less than $12,000. You might suggest that spending less than $12,000 during the year would be acceptable. This implies that spending less than what is budgeted on any line item is acceptable. If bringing in expenses under budget is not only acceptable but applauded, one could argue that spending less on missions than what's budgeted is also commendable.

Why did the board approve $12,000 for electricity? Is that based on the same consumption as the previous year plus an increase for inflation? How does the board know that in the previous year the electrical consumption was used prudently? Maybe the air conditioning wasn't turned up overnight and thus more electricity was used than was necessary. And how does it know what the inflation rate will be for the coming year?

Taking this one step further, let's suppose the fiscal year of a church in Scottsdale, Arizona ends in June. By the end of May, the amount budgeted for electricity has been reached. By virtue of what the board approved, no more electricity could be used, including what would be required to operate the air conditioning system. Within three minutes of the beginning of a Sunday service, we would discover that the board is far more concerned with a sanctuary conducive to worship than it is in complying with a $12,000 electrical budget.

Or imagine that the board has approved an office supply budget of $7500. The pastor, armed with the board's approval, purchases $7500 worth of pens and paper clips. Having spent the office supply budget in the first two weeks of the fiscal year, there's no money left to purchase paper to write on, and without paper, the paperclips are unnecessary. If we assume the pastor has a modicum of common sense, it's still possible that by the end of the eleventh month of the fiscal year, the office supply budget may have been reached. This may result in the staff not having sufficient supplies to do its job. The consequence will be that the staff takes the final month of the fiscal year off as a paid leave of absence.

While the above scenarios are ridiculous, many boards unwittingly approve such absurdity. Of course it doesn't want the required utilities turned off or cause the staff to operate without the required supplies. It values a comfortable building and an equipped office environment. But that's not what it approved.

Policy Governance is about organizational values being stated in the form of policies. When it comes to means, the board will reflect its values by limiting the means which the pastor can use to accomplish the board's stated ends.

Let's consider what a typical church board will value. One of those will be fiscal prudence. That's a nice way of saying that it doesn't want the church to go broke. As such, it may develop an Executive Limitation policy stating that in any fiscal year, the pastor cannot allow expenditures to exceed revenues. It may also have a policy which prohibits the pastor from operating without a long-term plan.

Is it possible for the board to value a balanced financial projection without concerning itself with the amount of overall annual expenses? Shouldn't the board value an administrative environment where employees are adequately resourced with the materials necessary to do their job without getting into the details of the cost or inventory of office supplies? Shouldn't the board receive data to show there's a plan for the church to be financially solvent without it having to decide whether the administrative assistant gets a two-percent or three-percent raise?

Unfortunately, boards can spend a lot of time going over the details of a budget—all with a view to making sure the church breaks even. Wouldn't it be easier to just state the bottom line value?

Look at the budget process through your new Policy Governance glasses. Board policies, including executive limitations, are based on your board's values. One of the Policy Governance lenses has your board seeing approvals as proactive rather than reactive. Instead of subjectively delving into means, your board is clear about what means are unacceptable. Once it has identified what it values and concomitantly what is unacceptable, it will be able to distinguish a good financial plan from a poor one when it sees it.

One of the things of which a board needs to be assured is that the information it receives is credible. At the risk of moving into a complex area outside the scope of this book, let me briefly address the matter of an audit committee. There's nothing within the Policy Governance system that restricts the use of any kind of committee, including an audit committee. However, any committee must be a committee of the board, which assists the board in its understanding of certain matters. These committees are not empowered separate from the board. In the case of an audit committee, it may have the authority to look into the credibility of the church's financial plan. It will have the latitude to review the numbers and underlying assumptions to assure the board that the projections are credible. It's not the job of an audit committee to advise the pastor or any of the staff regarding how money should be allocated.

Budgets aren't inherently evil. Every organization needs to have one. They've just been used for less than noble purposes. A board doesn't need to understand the whole budget, but it needs to know what it needs to understand about the budget.

This budget discussion provides a segue into one of the most critical and often overlooked principles of Policy Governance: monitoring.

17

HOW DOES THE BOARD MONITOR COMPLIANCE TO ITS DELEGATED AUTHORITY?

A long way back, we wrestled with the idea of the board giving away authority without giving away responsibility. We concluded that the secret was found in careful delegation. After that, we discovered how the board articulates the ends of the church—*what the beneficiaries will have or become* rather than *what the church will provide or do*. It then delegates its authority to the pastor for the accomplishment of those ends, allowing him or her to use any means except those which are specifically prohibited. The board clearly states what it has delegated and the expectations that go along with that delegated authority. However, planted in the collective hearts of the board is a solemn awareness that it has not and must not give away its responsibility. With that in mind, the board must have a formal way of ensuring that its expectations of the pastor, in light of the authority it has given away, are being met.

Another key principle of Policy Governance is that of monitoring. Monitoring must be regular and rigorous, with a view to discovering if the church is accomplishing the ends which are intended by its moral owners, while at the same time ensuring that none of the unacceptable means which the board has stated in its Executive Limitation policies are being employed. This is accomplished by means of a monitoring report. A monitoring report is developed by the pastor and has four components.

This report begins by stating the board's policy. Let's suppose your board states an executive limitation that the pastor must not allow expenditures to exceed revenues in any fiscal year. The board has stated a value of seeing that the ends of the church are accomplished without deficit spending. In developing a monitoring report, the pastor will essentially cut and paste this policy.

Your board has already decided it will accept any reasonable interpretation of this policy, so your pastor may interpret this policy as meaning there will be no deficit at the end of the fiscal year, but that there may be deficits throughout the year. If the church's fiscal year is the same as a calendar year, it would be reasonable to expect fewer and lower donations in January than December. While this interpretation makes sense, how does the board know that the church will be in a breakeven position by the end of the year? It will be of little consolation to find that the church is in a deficit position after the books are closed.

A good executive limitation which prevents the board from being caught off guard is one which states that the pastor shall not allow the board to be uninformed about any non-compliance or trends toward non-compliance. So if the financial conditions are such that the trend is toward non-compliance, the board needs to know. "We're doing fine" is not acceptable.

This leads us to the third component of a monitoring report, which is data. Never allow your pastor to provide a monitoring report that does not have data to demonstrate compliance with the board's executive limitation. If it's really important that your church doesn't end the year in a deficit, your board has the right and the responsibility, which it can't delegate, to know that such is not likely to happen.

IF IT'S REALLY IMPORTANT THAT YOUR CHURCH DOESN'T END THE YEAR IN A DEFICIT, YOUR BOARD HAS THE RIGHT AND THE RESPONSIBILITY, WHICH IT CAN'T DELEGATE, TO KNOW THAT SUCH IS NOT LIKELY TO HAPPEN.

One of the challenges for a pastor is providing data for something that hasn't happened. How can he or she prove a negative? If the executive limitations are stated in the negative—such as "must not cause or allow"—and that condition has not been caused or allowed, how can it be demonstrated? Let's suppose, with respect to the treatment of staff, that the pastor may not cause or allow conditions that are unlawful, unfair, undignified, disorganized, or unclear.

Now the pastor must reasonably interpret "unlawful, unfair, undignified, disorganized, and unclear." Unlawful, for example, could include conditions which violate applicable labor laws in the church's jurisdiction, such as hours of work, temperature of the office, or vacation time. Employee records and surveys or periodic environmental certifications could demonstrate that such conditions don't exist. Remember that any board value must be realizable—and if it can be realizable, there must be conditions in which that value is either realized or not realized. For example, it's not good enough to assume that management is treating staff with respect just because there's no indication or complaint indicating otherwise. There must be verifiable data that demonstrates that the staff is being treated with respect.

The final component of a monitoring report is the declaration of compliance. In the case where the pastor is non-compliant or partially compliant, a statement needs to be made indicating when he or she will move into compliance. If this timetable is accepted as reasonable by the board, it can adjust its monitoring timetable accordingly. If no such statement is provided, or the board finds the pastor's timetable unreasonable, it can impose a timetable of its own.

A monitoring report will be significantly different from other reports your board has previously received. It's not an informational report which elicits the typical board response: "That's interesting." It should be received in advance of the board meeting, providing sufficient time for each board member to review the report. In reviewing the report, a board member may come to an interim conclusion or have some concerns about an interpretation or certain data. These can then be raised at the meeting where the monitoring report is presented.

As each board member reviews the report, they should be asking four questions.

The first question is whether the policy being reported on is the current one. Sometimes a pastor will cut and paste a policy from a previous report which has since been changed.

The second question is whether the interpretation is complete and reasonable. If the Executive Limitation policy prohibits the pastor from causing or allowing poor working conditions, has that policy been interpreted? Remember that a reasonable interpretation is not what the board as a whole, or an individual board member, would prefer. It's only an interpretation which would be deemed reasonable by a reasonable person.

The third question each board member needs to ask is whether the data demonstrates compliance to the reasonable interpretation. Does it address the policy or just skate around the edges? For example, compliance with the board's value regarding the proscription of poor working conditions should not include the dates of the staff Christmas party.

The fourth question concerns whether the declaration of compliance is correct. In a case where the pastor has reported partial compliance or non-compliance, is the board willing to accept the proposed date for achieving compliance?

We've looked extensively at the importance of delegating authority while understanding that responsibility cannot be delegated. Your board has stated that its pastor can use any means to accomplish the ends of the church, except those it has prohibited. It sees the value of the Policy Governance principles, including monitoring reports. However, it will commit a common but fatal mistake if it doesn't regularly and rigorously monitor and follow up on the reports.

> IT WILL COMMIT A COMMON BUT FA- TAL MISTAKE IF IT DOESN'T REGULAR- LY AND RIGOROUSLY MONITOR AND FOLLOW UP ON THE REPORTS.

So far we've only talked about one method of monitoring, which involves an *internal report*. This method involves the pastor providing data which demonstrates compliance with the policies. The value of this type of report is that the pastor is aware in advance that policies will be monitored on a routine basis. Another value is that the board reminds itself to ensure compliance to those values which it deemed important enough to put a policy in place. And although this method of reporting is scheduled, regular, and routine, the board has the prerogative to monitor *any policy* at *any time* by *any means.*

So what other means or methods are there?

The board can monitor a policy through an *external report.* A common example of this is the external audit done by an auditing firm of which many churches are familiar. The type of inspection can also be done for such things as monitoring compliance to the board's limitation around the treatment of staff or information technology security.

A third type of monitoring is *direct inspection*. This is a method by which the board directly inspects compliance to a policy. It can do that as a whole, or more practically through a board-approved committee or taskforce. Keep in mind that this cannot be done unless the board as a whole approves the specifics of what is being monitored.

Policy Governance is a two-way street. In one lane, your pastor will have freedom to drive the church bus toward the board's stated ends and within the rules the board has put in place. In the next two chapters, we're going to look at how your board can stay on its side of the road by stating how it monitors its own values and how it treats its pastor.

18

HOW DOES A POLICY GOVERNANCE BOARD MONITOR ITSELF?

By now you understand that the role of a board is to govern on behalf of its moral owners. You know about the board's responsibility to formally and informally have its collective ears to the ground, listening to input from its owners. You understand that the board takes that input and translates it into ends which describe the results, changes, and benefits in the lives of an identified group of people. This includes determining the cost-benefit of those results. While it does that, it keeps in mind that there are good causes to which it will say no so the ends it has targeted will be accomplished. You're well aware of the difference between the ends and the means which are used to accomplish the ends. Your board has delegated authority to the pastor to see that the ends are accomplished using any means except those which the board has prohibited. You know it's important to evaluate the pastor only against the policies which the board has officially stated. This ensures that both the board and the pastor are clear that the success of the church equates to the success of the pastor.

Policy Governance has four sets of policies, all of which are developed by the board. We've already looked at Ends policies and Executive Limitation policies, along with the understanding that it is the pastor's responsibility to make sure the ends are accomplished and the unacceptable means avoided.

Means are not exclusive to the pastor. A board also has means by which it governs. In this chapter, we're going to look at the first of two sets of board means policies.

IS YOUR BOARD AS DISCIPLINED IN
EVALUATING ITS OWN PERFORMANCE
AS IT IS IN EVALUATING THE PASTOR?
IS YOUR CHURCH BOARD AS HARD ON
ITSELF AS IT IS ON ITS PASTOR?

So how's your board doing? It's got ends in place and executive limitations have been carefully thought through and put in writing. Authority has been clearly delegated and expectations are unmistakably clear. Monitoring reports are submitted by the pastor and the board reviews them carefully. The board as a whole makes decisions. It speaks with one voice and it knows what that voice is and how it's heard.

You have a firm handle on the organization, so let me pose the tough question: is your board as disciplined in evaluating its own performance as it is in evaluating the pastor? Is your church board as hard on itself as it is on its pastor?

We've looked at the means a pastor uses to accomplish the ends of the church. Now let's look at the board's means. These are laid out in what is referred to in the Policy Governance system as Governance Process policies. Let's take a high-level look at what areas should be covered in these policies.

Make sure the board is clear regarding its purpose. It's there to govern on behalf of its owners in assuring that what should happen (ends being accomplished) happens and what shouldn't happen (the use of unacceptable means) doesn't happen.

If you've sat on a board for more than twenty minutes, you'll know how easy it is to slide off the governance road and into the ditch by discussing means with the CEO. One board member asks (strongly suggests), "Have you given any thought to putting the announcements at the end of the service rather than the beginning?" The board will pose an idea that the next hire needs to be a pastor for seniors rather than a social media expert for the communications department. If you've discovered anything about Policy Governance, it's been its obsession with clarity. Never assume that the leader—or the board, for that matter—can clearly distinguish between a suggestion and an implied directive. Making suggestions or recommendations not only isn't the board's job, it's horribly counterproductive. It throws the door open to confusion and frustration for both the pastor and the board. Offering unsolicited advice isn't a good idea. There's enough work for the board to do.

If your board is acting on behalf of the members, adherents, and any other groups which it has identified as moral owners, how's it going? What information or data does it have which would give it confidence that the activities of the church are accomplishing the ends that the owners have in mind?

When a board convenes a meeting to connect with ownership, it will be helpful to provide the owners with a high-level overview of Policy Governance. However, it will lose people once it gets into too much detail. If you've had a hard enough time understanding the ends-means distinction, assume they will as well. They'll invariably talk about programming and other means issues. Listen carefully and patiently for the ends values which underlie those comments. As you do that, often ask questions which will draw out their deeper values as they relate to what you know as ends.

It's important that your board has the owner connection value in its Governance Process policies. This way, when it regularly reviews its policies, which reflect its values, it can know if it's staying on track with one of its jobs—that of connecting with owners.

Another Governance Process policy is the board's commitment to functioning legally. There may be some local, state, provincial, or federal laws requiring a board to do certain things. It's wise for a board to identify what those are and determine if it's compliant with those laws.

We know it's not a good idea to get caught up in a discussion about the preferences of individual board members, but it can easily happen. Even if your board has formally embraced Policy Governance, there'll invariably be some board members who use board time to offer opinions on their preferred means. Having a policy which clearly prohibits this tendency serves two purposes. The first is that having it written down, and later reviewed as a board, provides an opportunity to address the problem. The second advantage is that it's a gentle nudge that reminds each board member that a time will come when the individual behavior of each board member will be challenged. Of course, if a board member delves into means which the board has not limited, it's incumbent on the chair to address it and thus keep everyone focused on the board's agenda.[22]

All too often, there's an individual on a church board who tends to dominate a meeting. This person may have a long history with the church. Perhaps his family has been around for decades. Being well-off and a large donor can further exacerbate his sense of entitlement. When that happens, it's *always* the fault of the board. If it tolerates such bullying behavior, it deserves to have someone like that on the board. Since it surely values healthy interactions and deplores the dominance of one individual, it needs to have that value as one of its Governance Process policies. Once instituting it as one of its stated values, it needs to regularly review the policy to remind everyone of it and empower the chair to ensure that everyone gets a fair chance to speak and that everyone knows that deviation from the policy won't be tolerated.

When it comes to the board executive and board committees, here's another place to reinforce board holism. If your board has an executive committee, make sure you have a policy that ensures that the executive doesn't end up serving as a sub-board. It must not make decisions which are then essentially rubberstamped at the board meeting. The same principle applies to all other committees of the board. Boards sometimes assign tasks to a committee with no terms of reference and then accept the recommendations of the committee carte blanche. Instead, the board should ensure that its individual members' expertise serves to enhance the ability of the board as a whole to make good decisions.

In the first chapter, we looked at the challenge of boards having experts in many disciplines except governance. However, having board members with expertise isn't necessarily a bad thing. For example, there are times when an accountant or a lawyer can be an asset in rounding out the board's understanding of a particular matter. However, the board must avoid the temptation to default to the expertise of that person, and in doing so abandon its commitment to collective board decisions.

---

[22] Any concerns a board member may have about a means should be fully addressed by going to the policies and asking if those concerns are covered in a policy and adequately addressed in the relevant monitoring reports. If it is covered in a policy, board members should not become distracted by discussing the means which have not being limited within a policy.

There are more policies your board can consider as it develops its Governance Process policies. For now, there are three key points to underscore. The first is the importance of the board owning the values of being a good—no, a great—governing board. The second is developing policies that reflect those values. If it has a value, write it down. Finally, your board should intentionally schedule time to self-evaluate, ensuring that it's conducting itself in a manner consistent with what it values as stated in its Governance Process policies.

There's much more to be addressed in terms of board means, including the role of the chair, which some who use Policy Governance refer to as the chief governance officer (CGO). However, this chapter should get your board pointed in the right direction, specifically as it evaluates its own performance against its agreed upon values and the policies reflecting those values.

Your board has one other area where it needs to exercise self-discipline, and that's in the area of how it relates to its pastor. That's the subject of our next chapter.

19

How Should the Board Relate to Its Pastor?

I spent twenty-one years as an associate pastor. When I resigned, I had the requisite exit interview. One of the interviewers asked me to identify the low points of my time at the church. I immediately recognized that those times surrounded the departure of two senior pastors who had left under less than ideal conditions. One pastor had been terminated when the board arbitrarily developed expectations which had not been in place when he was hired. In the second instance, the pastor had a leadership style which resulted in some staff discreetly resigning while others groused in a tense work environment. In this second case, the board didn't have any policies regarding the unfair or unethical treatment of staff. The closest it came to becoming concerned was its gnawing suspicion that all wasn't healthy down the corporate hallway. In each situation, the board had nebulous values which it didn't explicitly state upfront, but it eventually demonstrated those values when the pastors were brusquely released.

This type of situation is far too common. Churches often have vague and diverse notions of what they expect or require of their pastors. Board members can't agree among themselves regarding their leadership expectations. As such, it's little wonder pastors walk through ministerial minefields. The board's targets are missed by pastors, less because they're moving targets and more because there are a variety of targets and pastors are left to figure out which ones to hit. Eventually there is only one target: the one on his or her back. When the arrow is buried deep and the pastor bleeds out, there will be some fallout, not the least of which is figuring out the political spin. Was it a resignation or a termination? Then there are the loyal parishioners who are upset, and the leadership continuity which is lost. The pastor's family becomes collateral damage as they lose their church home. Many pastors decide it isn't worth the fight and end up driving a truck where they're treated with some respect. Churches too often treat their pastors in ways they would never dream of treating anyone else.

And it's all so unnecessary. However, let me get off this ranting road and back onto the freeway of stoic objectivity.

> CHURCHES TOO OFTEN TREAT THEIR PASTORS IN WAYS THEY WOULD NEVER DREAM OF TREATING ANYONE ELSE.

This chapter will deal with the second set of policies, often called Board-Management Delegation policies. Within the context of your church, you may want to refer to them as Board-Pastor Delegation policies. These are policies which the church board imposes upon itself in terms of how it will delegate authority to its pastor, set its expectations, and monitor compliance.

One of the values upon which the Policy Governance system is built is that of *role precision* between the board and the CEO, and one of the ways by which a Policy Governance church board ensures this clarity is by having only one employee. To this person the board delegates authority to use any means to accomplish the ends of the church, except those the board has prohibited. A board using Policy Governance will be fastidious in bifurcating the role of the pastor from the role of the board. There will be no overlap or ambiguity.

If that is such a huge value—and it must be—then it makes sense that the value is stated in the form of an unequivocally clear policy. This is put in place through a formally passed motion of the board, and it becomes the only way by which a board officially communicates with its pastor. A temptation for the board is to agree with this official position but then cheat by making invited suggestions or offering words of unsolicited advice. Sometimes the board will know better than to use these words, so it will make a hint. Hinting doesn't count; advice doesn't count; a suggestion doesn't count. Only officially passed motions count. Not only do hints, advice, and suggestions not count, they're counterproductive and confusing. So don't do it.

If delegation is to be clear, it must be clear regarding what is delegated and to whom, and it must also be clear who is doing the delegating. There can only be one delegating voice, and that voice is the voice of the board. This means that individual board members, including the chair, must not provide instructions or direction. The same principle applies to committees of the board. On very rare occasions, the board may specifically authorize or direct a committee or individual to give instructions, but that should be the exception rather than the rule.

I was the chair of a mission organization for a number of years. I'd led the transition to Policy Governance and as such was careful not to interfere with the work of the executive director, who was the only employee of the organization. He was well-schooled in the principle that not only does the board not give instructions to the executive director (other than those contained in the board's policies), but neither does the chair. On a few occasions, he faced some decisions and wanted my input. He usually invited this by making a phone call and would begin by saying, "I'm calling you as a friend." In doing so, he was subtly stating that he was free to ignore whatever input I provided. This worked well because we have a good personal and professional relationship, but the practice is fraught with danger and should be rarely used and carefully guarded.

This Policy Governance principle is quite simple. Only one voice delegates, and that is the voice of the board as a whole. In a previous chapter, we learned that the voice of the board is spoken through its motions. That's the only voice to which the pastor has any responsibility to listen. The pastor is the only employee of the board, and therefore he or she is the only one to whom the board gives instructions. There's only one delegator, and that's the board as a whole. There's only one delegatee, and that's the pastor. There's only one set of messages to the pastor, and those are contained in the Ends policies and the Executive Limitation policies. In the case of your church, the pastor is free to use any reasonable interpretation of the board's policies.

With this clear and simple relationship in place, let's look at some implications. The board has agreed to accept any reasonable interpretation of its policies, even if an interpretation isn't the one preferred by the board or any member of the board. That's a tough swallow for board members who've been used to giving direction to the pastor and overturning ideas which they don't like. If you don't think that will be a challenge, wait until the board is informed that the choir is being disbanded and the organ is being sold. Yes, *that* choir, which you and your ancestors have sung in since Bethlehem. Yes, *that* organ, with little brass plates identifying donors who have long gone Home. Try having your board turn over the budget process to the pastor. You may find it's easier to talk your four-year-old into giving up his soother or talk your ten-year-old into throwing out her worn-out teddy bear. But like an adhesive bandage on a hairy stomach, there's only one way to get it off—fast.

By the way, just one more thing.[23] You remember the annual performance evaluation? Under Policy Governance, the typical performance evaluation is gone with the soother, the teddy bear, and the tape.

Let's have a look at those monitoring reports again. We have all the board's values embedded in its Ends policies and Executive Limitation policies. The board has clearly stated what should happen and what shouldn't happen. The pastor has provided a reasonable interpretation of the board's policies, along with the data to demonstrate compliance to those policies. The board can review the monitoring reports to see whether the pastor has been out of compliance in any area. If so, the board can require the pastor to make adjustments to move back into compliance.

What can the board evaluate apart from that? Its only instructions have been through the policies. Therefore, it must not have expectations of the pastor which are not contained in those policies. Many organizations have a Board-Management Delegation policy stating that "the board will view CEO performance as identical to organizational performance, so that organizational accomplishment of board-stated ends and avoidance of board-proscribed means will be viewed as

---

[23] "By the way" means that what's coming is extremely important and something you likely won't want to hear.

successful CEO performance." So if your church is accomplishing its ends and no prohibited means are being used, the church is obviously successful and therefore the pastor is successful.

Imagine a church where the pastor isn't surprised or broadsided by a subjective or arbitrary performance evaluation. Wouldn't it be freeing for your pastor to know with absolute clarity the criteria against which he or she is being evaluated? Success is clearly defined, and therefore so is failure. Subjective opinions of your pastor's performance are gone. Eradicated from a board's vocabulary are terms such as "I'm not comfortable with…" or "I just feel that…" or "I wish that…" or "I'm not sure about…" If those terms ever arise, they must come up in the context of developing proactive policies.

This type of clarity is what your pastor needs and deserves, and this is the type of clarity your board can provide.

20

WHAT ARE THE DRAWBACKS
TO POLICY GOVERNANCE?

I took the car for a test drive as the salesperson espoused the virtues of the vehicle. The pitch was such that I couldn't imagine why anyone would buy any other model than the one I would have to finance. As we headed back to the showroom, he offered to answer any questions I might have. His sales talk should have rendered every potential question irrelevant, but it didn't.

"What reasons would the salesperson of another car manufacturer give me for not buying this car?" I probed.

"Hmmm," he pondered. "No one's ever asked me that before."

There must be some reasons why a church board would not want to buy the Policy Governance model. Many have considered implementing Policy Governance and decided against it for various reasons. Some have heard negative comments about the system and therefore aren't even interested in taking it for a test drive. Others have tried it and didn't like it. So let's look at each of the ten principles and identify the potential drawbacks.

The International Policy Governance Association, in listing the ten principles of Policy Governance (see Appendix A), uses the analogy of an old-time watch that is more than the sum of its parts. For the next while, we're going to take the watch apart and lay each of its ten components on the board table. We're going to take each part and find out why we wouldn't want that piece as part of the governance watch. To make sure we have no bent or poorly constructed pieces, we'll get a watch from the factory.

With that in mind, let's take a look at each of the Policy Governance principles as listed in Appendix A, and quote directly from it. Then we can be well-informed as we decide which pieces are extraneous to the functioning of our governance timepiece.

Principle 1: Ownership

The board exists to act as the informed voice and agent of the owners, whether they are owners in a legal or moral sense. All owners are stakeholders, but not all stakeholders are owners, only those whose position in relation to an organization is equivalent to the position of shareholders in a for-profit-corporation.

Drawback: This principle doesn't allow a board to view itself as the ultimate owner.

If a board believes it has no legal or moral obligation to any individual or body—which Policy Governance refers to as moral owners—then this part can be put aside. If a board has any governance role at all, it governs only on behalf of its own interests. Even if it has been appointed or elected by a body of people, the need to hear from the electing body stops at the point the board is elected. There will be no implied requirement that a board should interact with, or receive input from, those who appointed or elected it.

Principle 2: Position of Board

The board is accountable to owners that the organization is successful. As such it is not advisory to staff but an active link in the chain of command. All authority in the staff organization and in components of the board flows from the board.

Drawback: This principle prevents a board or any member of a board from providing direction to its staff.

If a board recognized that there's a body of people who owns the ministry of a local church and it governs on their behalf, then wouldn't it be accountable to some moral ownership to stay on top of things by giving advice, suggestions, counsel, and direction to the staff? After all, staff works for a board, so everyone is ostensibly an employee of that board or any board member. Add to that the expertise of people on a board, of which the pastor needs to take advantage. Why would these fountains of wisdom and knowledge go untapped?

Then at times, a board might offer advice to its pastor, or an individual board member with expertise in a certain area may provide some direction. Whether the input is advisory or directive in nature is something a good pastor should intuitively understand. The Policy Governance stand on the position of a board is a drawback to any board that wants arbitrary fluidity between the role of a board and that of its pastor.

Principle 3: Board Holism

The authority of the board is held and used as a body. The board speaks with one voice in that instructions are expressed by the board as a whole. Individual board members have no authority to instruct staff.

Drawback: This principle doesn't allow individual board members to function independently.

The problem with the Policy Governance principle of board holism and the one-voice concept is that it requires every board member to uphold a decision of the board even if that board member doesn't agree with it.

Board holism doesn't permit the board to give direction to the pastor or one of the staff by flashing their board member card.

If this principle wasn't part of the Policy Governance system, it would free an individual board member to take the position that while a board as a whole has said one thing, he or she sees it differently and therefore is free to act according to his or her own opinion. Every board member would be free to voice their opinions outside a board meeting in the same way it could at a board table. After all, what happened to First Amendment rights? The overall board message may not be clear, concise, or consistent, but everyone will know where each board member stands. This allows the one with the most persuasive argument or loudest voice to carry the message.

Principle 4: Ends Policies

The board defines in writing its expectations about the intended effects to be produced, the intended recipients of those effects, and the intended worth (cost-benefit or priority) of the effects. These are Ends policies. All decisions made about effects, recipients, and worth are ends decisions. All decisions about issues that do not fit the definition of ends are means decisions. Hence in Policy Governance, means are simply not ends.

Drawback: The principle of ends is too nebulous and undermines the importance of church ministries.

The Policy Governance principle of ends is counterintuitive to the ways by which the church has traditionally defined success. This principle denigrates the idea that a church exists to provide worship services, outreach events, and discipleship programming. It doesn't allow a church to mark success just by increased attendance. It doesn't let a church assume that attendees are benefitting from the programs of the church. It seems to implicitly attack the biblical value of God giving the increase.

A church is doing fine if it provides programming for all ages and continues to preach the gospel, and as such the concept of ends serves no real purpose. The exponential growth of a church is sufficient in determining the blessing of God, so the ends principle is an unwelcome complication. Ends appear to diminish the value of creative programs, staff initiative, and hard work. They don't give due credit to creativity, initiative, and diligence, which should count for something even if they don't work in the long run.

Principle 5: Board Means Policies

The board defines in writing the job results, practices, delegation style, and discipline that make up its own job. These are board means decisions, categorized as Governance Process policies and Board-Management Delegation policies.

Drawback: This principle doesn't allow for board agility.

In the Policy Governance system, there are policies that define and restrict the board's behavior. Admittedly there are advantages to this, as it assures reasonable expectations of attendance, preparedness, and decorum. However, Policy Governance goes far beyond that.

The idea of connecting with moral owners is great, but it requires initiative and creativity. A board must first decide who its moral owners are—and who they are not. Having landed on that, how will it connect with the owners? What if there is more than one group of owners? How does the board effectively connect with each group? And finally, what does it do with the feedback it gets from the owners? This is starting to sound like a lot of work and hassle.

Then there's that matter of never weighing in on means, except to the extent that it limits those means which are unacceptable. For board members who have felt free to weigh in on the means its pastor uses to accomplish the ends, this part will be tough to fit into the watch.

Policy Governance goes further by limiting the board's own behavior regarding how it relates to its pastor. Imagine what would happen if a board imposed written limitations in terms of how it interacts with the pastor in or out of a board meeting. Using a football analogy, how's a board supposed to make audible calls when it has locked itself down by its own policies? Furthermore, this Policy Governance principle only serves to paralyze individual board members from giving unilateral instructions to its employees. Ultimately, a board would be compelled to evaluate its pastor based only on stated policies and expectations. Gone would be the freedom to offer an arbitrary assessment of his or her performance. The annual evaluation process would be limited to an appraisal based on clearly stated and mutually understood expectations.

A board which uses Policy Governance is supposed to invest time and money into ongoing training and education for itself. It brings in the experts, who inform a board about trends in church dynamics or issues the church will be facing in the next five to ten years. This information in turn would force a board to rethink its ends. Goodness knows it will take a board long enough to settle on certain Ends policies. Now more time needs to be spent. People are busy. It's hard enough to recruit board members without scaring them off with a governance system of self-discipline and a rigorous push for ongoing improvement.

By placing those kinds of demands on itself, a Policy Governance board will have to routinely ask itself if it's behaving in a specific manner that's consistent with its own expectations. It doesn't allow itself to sidestep its own rules or arbitrarily change them because they're not expedient.

Surely a governance watch can operate well enough without this part.

Principle 6: Executive Limitations Policies
The board defines in writing its expectations about the means of the operational organization. However, rather than prescribing board-chosen means—which would enable the CEO to escape accountability for attaining ends, these policies define limits on operational means, thereby placing boundaries on the authority granted to the CEO. In effect, the board describes those means that would be unacceptable even if they were to work. These are Executive Limitations policies.

Drawback: The principle of executive limitations potentially gives too much or too little authority to a pastor.

A healthy board wants to strike a good balance between rubberstamping and micromanaging. This principle doesn't allow a board to move its slider of involvement along the rubberstamp-micromanagement continuum as it sees fit.

A board of this nature cannot embrace the principle of executive limitations. Virtually every executive limitation uses language such as "shall not allow," "shall not cause," or other phrases which prohibit or limit the means used by its CEO. A Policy Governance board, by virtue of the rules it imposes upon itself, isn't allowed to be directive. It can define the ends to be accomplished, but it can't tell the pastor how to do it. How's a board supposed to control an organization when it has no input into how things are done. This principle allows a pastor to use any means he or she wants to accomplish the church's ends, unless the board explicitly prohibits it. Relinquishing control of operations by not being able to direct how the pastor does the ministry is too big a pill to swallow. It would be better if a board just arbitrarily told its pastor how to do his or her job. "Arbitrarily" obviously doesn't mean giving direction for everything, because that would be impractical. For example, a board wouldn't dictate which washroom supplies to buy or what day of the week the auditorium should be vacuumed, but it needs to have input on the bigger issues. Doing so requires flexibility on the part of a board—and its pastor.

From time to time, there'll be some disagreement among various board members as to what the bigger issues are. When that happens, a board will need to take some time to decide so that it can delineate every issue, thus making sure the pastor knows which are the bigger issues for the board to deal with and which fall to the pastor to exercise his or her own judgement. A board then can develop a very complete and comprehensive list of what the CEO *can* do, so he or she can't do anything wrong. All the pastor will be required to do in this case is hit the target of understanding the board's position on the bigger issues.

Principle 7: Policy Sizes

The board decides its policies in each category first at the broadest, most inclusive level. It further defines each policy in descending levels of detail until reaching the level of detail at which it is willing to accept any reasonable interpretation by the applicable delegatee of its words thus far. Ends, Executive Limitations, Governance Process, and Board-Management Delegation policies are exhaustive in that they establish control over the entire organization, both board and staff. They replace, at the board level, more traditional documents such as mission statements, strategic plans and budgets.

Drawback: The principle of policy sizes is too restrictive for a board. Policy boards (not be confused with Policy Governance boards) work hard to make sure their policies are current and detailed. As soon as something comes up of which a board may not approve, it can write a policy to address the matter. This reactively blocks the CEO from going in any direction which is not acceptable to a board. This frees a board from having to think proactively and comprehensively about its values and addressing those values in the form of a policy.

The Policy Governance principle of policy sizes isn't about how many or how few words are contained in a policy, but rather about its breadth and depth. The challenge with this principle is that the original policy must be broad and the subsequent policies provide an increasing level of detail in relation to the broader policy. A board which uses Policy Governance doesn't have the liberty to develop random policies without tying those policies to a greater value. It doesn't have the option of writing policies as a way of expressing its preferences. The board doesn't have the choice to say, "That's not what we meant," or reactively change the policy.

The idea of policy sizes forces a systematic and strategic development of policies that move from a general value to one which is more specific, and then releases the pastor to use any reasonable interpretation. After establishing a policy, this principle doesn't allow a board to subsequently state its preferences or suggest a particular means.

If a board wants to stay one step ahead of the pastor—or in some cases, no more than one step behind—this principle of strategic and intentional policy sizes will not allow it to be reactionary.

Principle 8: Clarity and Coherence of Delegation

The identification of any delegatee must be unambiguous as to authority and responsibility. No subparts of the board, such as committees or officers, can be given jobs that interfere with, duplicate, or obscure the job given to the CEO.

Drawback: This principle limits a board's flexibility.

If a board is the employer of its CEO, as the Policy Governance system would maintain, then shouldn't anyone connected with that board be able to decide at any time to provide input or direction to the CEO? Shouldn't a board be allowed to delegate its authority to whomever it likes? And if it's a board's prerogative to delegate authority, shouldn't it be able to take back that authority from time to time or delegate it to another person or a committee? Wouldn't it be better for a board if it had flexibility to delegate and then override that delegation? Sure, a pastor may be occasionally surprised or frustrated, but as the employee of a board, that goes with the territory. Besides, he or she is still being paid to do the job.

What if a board member has an idea about changing one of the service times? Shouldn't that person have the freedom to put forward that idea for further board discussion? If a board puts out some ideas, the pastor should be able to intuitively decide if the input is mandatory or optional. He or she should also be able to figure out if it reflects the view of the board or just one person. If two people have input, the pastor may want to meet with each individual to find out how strongly they feel.

As with some of the other Policy Governance principles, this principle demands clarity by ruling out the ability of the board to make arbitrary changes.

Principle 9: Any Reasonable Interpretation
More detailed decisions about ends and operational means are delegated to the CEO if there is one. If there is no CEO, the board must delegate to two or more delegatees, avoiding overlapping expectations or causing confusion about the authority of various managers. In the case of board means, delegation is to the CGO unless part of the delegation is explicitly directed elsewhere, for example, to a committee. The delegatee has the right to use any reasonable interpretation of the applicable board policies.

Drawback: This doesn't allow a board to write a policy *and* interpret it.

A board writes a policy, and then the pastor gets to tell the board what it meant? Not a chance. A board needs to maintain the right to decide what it intended when it wrote a policy. For example, if a church board wants to limit its pastor by stating that its capital assets cannot be exposed to irrecoverable loss, it should also be able to decide that the pastor must have insurance, including the amount of the policy and the insurance company from which it needs to be purchased. After all, that's what it meant. To allow the pastor to use any reasonable interpretation results in a board giving up that flexibility. Even if it accepts the principle of any reasonable interpretation, surely it must reserve the right to dismiss an interpretation if some or all members of the board don't like it. It's critical that a board controls its pastor by ensuring that it's able to interpret its own policies.

Principle 10: Monitoring

The board must monitor organizational performance against previously stated Ends policies and Executive Limitations policies. Monitoring is for the purpose of discovering if the organization achieved a reasonable interpretation of these board policies. The board must therefore judge the CEO's interpretation for its reasonableness, and the data demonstrating the accomplishment of the interpretation. The ongoing monitoring of board's Ends and Executive Limitations policies constitutes the CEO's performance evaluation.

Drawback: A competent leader shouldn't have to be monitored.

This sounds like babysitting. It should be good enough for a board to clearly delineate the ends to be accomplished and the means to be avoided and trust that these will be complied with. The work of having a pastor interpret the policies and regularly provide data to a board seems like too many reports. Furthermore, if these monitoring reports were meaningful, they would need to be reviewed by a board. If a board doesn't like the outcome of one of its policies after a monitoring report is submitted, it doesn't have the freedom to retroactively change it.

This piece of the watch is not just extraneous, it appears to do more harm than good. The board ends up being stuck with what it gets.

In Summary

So there you have it: ten reasons why a board may not like the Policy Governance system. We began by using the analogy of a watch. If you've gotten this far into the book, hopefully you have found lots of reasons to want the Policy Governance watch. The tough part is that you only need to leave one part out to render the watch useless.

One of the most common critiques of the Policy Governance system is the one-size-fits-all idea. Keep in mind that different critics may have different interpretations of one-size-fits-all. With that in mind, let me interpret my understanding of it.

Some detractors have a problem with the concept that every principle of the Policy Governance system is essential. Some suggest that the system can work without using all the principles. In looking at the drawbacks to

> THERE IS NOT ONE PRINCIPLE OF POLICY GOVERNANCE THAT CAN BE REMOVED WITHOUT IMPACTING SOME, IF NOT ALL, THE OTHERS.

the principles, you will have seen that the Policy Governance system isn't built on independent plug-and-play principles. Having decided to leave out one principle—or two, or three—a board has potentially compromised some or all of the remaining principles. There is not one principle of Policy Governance that can be removed without impacting some, if not all, the others.

For example, once board holism is taken out, each of the other nine principles is in jeopardy. Each board member gets to decide who the owners are and what instructions are provided to a pastor. A board can't govern on behalf of owners if there are no recognized owners. It can't delegate authority to the pastor for accomplishing ends and then let the pastor off the hook by telling him or her how to do it. A board as a whole can't delegate if individual board members can delegate what or how they want.

In the event that your board concludes that:

1. It is accountable to its legal and moral owners,
2. It doesn't exist to advise or tell the qualified pastor it has hired how to do his or her job,

3. It's unacceptable for renegade board members to seek to undermine official board decisions,
4. The church doesn't exist to employ people and administrate programs,
5. It should be disciplined and principled rather than random and arbitrary,
6. It has hired a competent pastor who shouldn't be confused by directions from individual board members,
7. Its policies should be clear, consistent, comprehensive, and sequential,
8. There should be no confusion as to who is responsible for operations,
9. Micromanaging is never a good idea and always an impossible task, or
10. If it's important enough to have expectations, then it's important enough to make sure the expectations are met...

...then why not implement Policy Governance?

21

POLICY GOVERNANCE
ISN'T THE SILVER BULLET

After my annual check-up, the doctor sternly recommended that I start going to the gym. I told him about my busy schedule and whatever other excuses came to mind, but eventually I agreed.

"How often do I need to go?" I asked.

"At least three times per week and for at least an hour at a time."

At a follow-up appointment, he asked how things were going at the gym. I was glad I'd been going the requisite three times per week. He still didn't look too pleased. Somehow the changes he had hoped to see weren't there.

"What kind of machines are you using?" he probed.

"The juice machine and the snack machine," I proudly replied.

Eventually he had to point out that just going to the gym wouldn't help. I actually had to do something while I was there.

As dumb as that sounds, there are people who think implementing Policy Governance is the cure for all governance problems.

In the previous chapter, we took the Policy Governance watch apart, laying its pieces out on our board table. Hopefully you discovered that every part is necessary, and that by taking out one part, the watch won't perform the function for which it was intended.

While I am a strong proponent of the Carver watch, I'm not being paid to sell it. I believe in it. I wear it. I tell time by it. And yes, sometimes it frustrates me. Its alarm goes off and wakes me up. It tells me the time when I wish the time was different. It has its shortcomings. It tells time with incredible accuracy, but it doesn't get me to my appointments on time. Its alarm goes off, but it doesn't get me out of bed.

I've shown the Policy Governance watch to mission agencies, charities, Bible camps, and churches. Most love the watch, but some have found it wanting.

A pastor once spoke with a friend who had suggested the Carver model. Later, that pastor read my book, *A Guide to Governing Charities*, and was convinced this is what his church board needed. The church's board meetings were protracted, as directors wandered with seeming aimlessness in and out of out of various topics and issues. Some board members were fascinated by the discussions, some were intrigued, while others failed miserably at their efforts not to look bored. These meanderings led the board to becoming bogged down. In attempts to salvage something from the time and passion invested, motions would be passed. The board randomly addressed certain issues while ignoring others. It obsessed over the budget, but responded to year-end deficits with, "Oops… we'll get it next year."

One of the board members, originally from South America, was confident he knew how the church could serve in that part of the world. Another board member had a degree in human resources and periodically imposed his expertise on the pastor.

The board agreed to engage my services beginning with an introduction to Policy Governance. This led to their decision to proceed with its implementation. I then facilitated some sessions in the development of Governance Process, Board-Pastor Relationship, and Executive Limitation policies. Later we worked on developing Ends policies. I followed up by offering to coach the board and the pastor to heighten the likelihood of their success.

After a few meetings, the board assured me it sufficiently understood Policy Governance and that it didn't need my input. I was on a contract basis for the year, so lest you think money was an issue, it wasn't. I followed up by having two meetings with the board chair, offering hints and even outright advice. But to no avail.

I later met with the pastor, who was all too aware that his role and the role of the board were blurred, that boundaries had been violated and the policies by which the board had agreed to conduct itself were being ignored. Then new board members came on who had no understanding or appreciation of Policy Governance. A few pieces of the watch were still on the board room table, but most were lost within the covers of forgotten Policy Governance manuals.

It took two years for the pastor to resign. By that time, the board was unhappy with him. Some of its grievances were clear violations of certain executive limitations, including some policies which had never been monitored. However, many of its criticisms of the pastor had nothing to do with anything it had laid out in terms of policies. The denunciations were chronic, vague, and nebulous. The board even offered him a six-month probationary period during which he could prove himself. I'm sure neither the pastor nor the board had any idea what a successful probationary period would look like, never mind the attendant results.

That church board will purport that going to the Policy Governance gym didn't result in it becoming healthier. Maybe it wasn't the right gym, the right equipment, or the right trainer. In any event, the church isn't going back to the Policy Governance gym anytime soon.

So what went wrong? A turnover of board members and the pastor being released renders an empirical conclusion virtually impossible. However, based on other cases, we could extrapolate some possibilities. In all likelihood, they will be reduced to two foundational problems.

The first problem is that the church board didn't see Policy Governance as a whole new game. It saw it as just another way of doing board governance. It seemed like a good idea, but it never saw the need for radical change. Unless it saw Policy Governance as a different game and not just some nuanced changes to an old game, it was destined to fail. The field was a different shape, and the equipment was different. Baseball can't be played while wearing skates. Proactive policies must replace reactive decisions. Micromanagement and rubberstamping are not practices to be avoided, because Policy Governance doesn't allow a board to do either.

The second problem is that the board wasn't willing to embrace the discipline required in overcoming the instincts of most traditional board members. It isn't just a matter of eating one less piece of pie or walking fifteen minutes a day; it's a complete change of lifestyle, and that's not easy for a board which has never exercised self-discipline at the board table.

Some blame needs to lie with the trainer—that's me. What mistakes did I make and how could I have instructed the board in a way which would have increased the likelihood of success?

At the outset, the shift to Policy Governance was initiated by a charismatic leader. In many ways, he was the de facto chair of the board. When he suggested the Policy Governance system to the board, it accepted the idea. Early in the process, he left his position at the church, and with his departure went the one championing the implementation of Policy Governance.

THE NATURE OF THE POLICY GOVERNANCE SYSTEM IS SUCH THAT IT WON'T SURVIVE WHEN THERE'S A SINGLE ADVOCATE

The nature of the Policy Governance system is such that it won't survive when there's a single advocate, whether that's the pastor, the board chair, or someone else on the board. In this example, the departure of the pastor certainly contributed to the ineffective implementation of the system. However, his departure likely only hastened the inevitable failure.

I failed, in that I facilitated a process that didn't have the buy-in of the whole board. Before a board agrees to move ahead with Policy Governance, it needs to have more than the tacit support of its members. There needs to be freedom on the part of the board to provide pushback, oppose the concept, and review the drawbacks. Sometimes boards are so frustrated with the way things have gone in the past that anything different will be appealing. Other boards can be culturally compliant which results in support of something they don't really understand.

Sometimes, after a robust conversation about implementing Policy Governance, a board is divided. Some may be fully confident in moving ahead with the system. Others may be equally as adamant that using the Policy Governance system is regressive. Some may be willing to give it a try but aren't altogether sold. In the end, it will come down to how the board votes. If according to its rules, a majority affirms the motion to implement the system, a board can move forward. However, this needs to be done with the utmost care. This isn't a simple board decision about a motion; it goes to the heart of how the board will be moving forward in the future.

I spent a weekend introducing Policy Governance to the board of a denomination. At the end of the meeting, the chair was ready to entertain a motion to have the board implement the system. I could tell that the majority would vote in favor, but there were one or two long-time board members who were reticent. I suggested that the vote be postponed until the next board meeting. The postponement resulted in the board defeating the motion. While the majority was ready to move ahead, they saw the perils of doing so when some were still struggling with the idea. I believe they were wise not to push it, but rather to be patient. Policy Governance requires such a great degree of ownership and discipline that it needs everyone pulling in the same direction. When that doesn't happen, it's difficult to successfully carry out all the principles of the system.

When a board contemplates moving to Policy Governance, it can result in some board members immediately stepping down or serving out their terms. Those who are more comfortable with the traditional model may see how excited others are about the value Policy Governance can bring to the board. When that happens, some board members will step aside. Recently, a board member of a mission organization told me of a situation where this happened rather dramatically. When the decision was made to move ahead with Policy Governance, one board member closed his laptop, offered a verbal resignation, and walked out. Departures are usually not so immediate or intense. Some board members will serve out the balance of their term and quietly move on.

If your board is considering Policy Governance, don't let a consultant sell you on it. It's not the silver bullet. Nor should your board implement the Policy Governance system just because the consultant thinks it's the only way.

I'm convinced that Policy Governance, if implemented carefully, will increase the effectiveness and efficiency of your board. Passive attendance at the Policy Governance gym doesn't make you a healthier board. Only its active engagement in the employment of all the Policy Governance principles will contribute to excellence in owner-accountable governance.

IN CLOSING

...I will build my church, and the gates of hell shall not prevail against it. (Matthew 16:18, ESV)

There are approximately three hundred thousand Christian churches in the United States[24] and a further nineteen thousand in Canada.[25] That makes for a lot of jobsites where God is building His church. What a privilege to be part of the greatest construction project ever to take place in the universe!

My goal in writing this book has been to provide a framework to clear away any governance rubble so workers are freed up to build with efficiency. Most importantly, I want to assist in constructing this edifice while acknowledging that if the Lord doesn't build, those who try to build will do so in vain (see Psalm 127:1).

---

[24] *Hartford Institute for Religion Research*, "Fast Facts About American Religion." Date of access: March 4, 2015 (http://hirr.hartsem.edu/research/fastfacts/fast_facts.html).

[25] *Canadian Church Directory*, "Looking for a Church in Canada?" Date of access: March 4, 2015 (http://churchdirectory.ca/).

Appendix A

Policy Governance® Official Source Document[26]
This official document lays out what *is* and what *is not* Policy Governance.

Why a Source Document?
A "source" is a point of origin. A source document is a "fundamental document or record on which subsequent writings, compositions, opinions, beliefs, or practices are based." (Websters)

Without a simply expressed clear point of source, interpretations, opinions, writings and implementations may intentionally or unintentionally diverge from the originating intent and ultimately be undifferentiated. The point of source ("authoritative source") is John Carver, the creator of Policy Governance, with Miriam Carver his fellow master teacher.

Without a simply expressed clear source document, Policy Governance is not reliably grounded and not transferable as a paradigm of governance. It is left vulnerable to interpretation, adaptation and impotence. This document has been produced by the International Policy Governance Association and approved by John and Miriam Carver as being true to source.

What Policy Governance Is *Not*:
1. Policy Governance is not a specific board structure. It does not dictate board size, specific officers, or require a CEO.

---

[26] Produced by International Policy Governance Association in consultation with John and Miriam Carver, 2005, 2007, 2011. Policy Governance® is a registered service mark of John Carver. Used with permission. Copying permitted if attributed to source. If referenced as source document, must reference entire document and, if copied, be copied in its entirety. Policy Governance® is an internationally registered service mark of John Carver. Registration is only to ensure accurate description of the model rather than for financial gain. The model is available free to all with no royalties or licence fees for its use. The authoritative website for Policy Governance is www.carvergovernance.com.

While it gives rise to principles for committees, it does not prohibit committees nor require specific committees.

2. Policy Governance is not a set of individual "best practices" or tips for piecemeal improvement.

3. Policy Governance does not dictate what a board should do or say about group dynamics, methods of needs assessment, basic problem solving, fund raising, or managing change.

4. Policy Governance does not limit human interaction or stifle collective or individual thinking.

What Policy Governance Is:

Policy Governance is a comprehensive set of integrated principles that, when consistently applied, allows governing boards to realize owner-accountable organizations.

Starting with recognition of the fundamental reasons that boards exist and the nature of board authority, Policy Governance integrates a number of unique principles designed to enable accountable board leadership.

The Ten Principles of Policy Governance

1. Ownership: The board exists to act as the informed voice and agent of the owners, whether they are owners in a legal or moral sense. All owners are stakeholders, but not all stakeholders are owners, only those whose position in relation to an organization is equivalent to the position of shareholders in a for-profit-corporation.

2. Position of Board: The board is accountable to owners that the organization is successful. As such it is not advisory to staff but an active link in the chain of command. All authority in the staff organization and in components of the board flows from the board.

3. Board Holism: The authority of the board is held and used as a body. The board speaks with one voice in that instructions are expressed by the board as a whole. Individual board members have no authority to instruct staff.

4. Ends Policies: The board defines in writing its expectations about the intended effects to be produced, the intended recipients of those effects, and the intended worth (cost-benefit or priority) of the effects. These are Ends policies. All decisions made about effects, recipients, and worth are ends decisions. All decisions about issues that do not fit the definition of ends are means decisions. Hence in Policy Governance, means are simply not ends.

5. Board Means Policies: The board defines in writing the job results, practices, delegation style, and discipline that make up its own job. These are board means decisions, categorized as Governance Process policies and Board- Management Delegation policies.

6. Executive Limitations Policies: The board defines in writing its expectations about the means of the operational organization. However, rather than prescribing board-chosen means— which would enable the CEO to escape accountability for attaining ends, these policies define limits on operational means, thereby placing boundaries on the authority granted to the CEO. In effect, the board describes those means that would be unacceptable even if they were to work. These are Executive Limitations policies.

7. Policy Sizes: The board decides its policies in each category first at the broadest, most inclusive level. It further defines each policy in descending levels of detail until reaching the level of detail at which it is willing to accept any reasonable interpretation by the applicable delegatee of its words thus far. Ends, Executive Limitations, Governance Process, and Board-Management Delegation policies are exhaustive in that they establish control over the entire organization, both board and staff. They replace, at the board level, more traditional documents such as mission statements, strategic plans and budgets.

8. Clarity and Coherence of Delegation: The identification of any delegatee must be unambiguous as to authority and

responsibility. No subparts of the board, such as committees or officers, can be given jobs that interfere with, duplicate, or obscure the job given to the CEO.

9. Any Reasonable Interpretation: More detailed decisions about ends and operational means are delegated to the CEO if there is one. If there is no CEO, the board must delegate to two or more delegatees, avoiding overlapping expectations or causing confusion about the authority of various managers. In the case of board means, delegation is to the CGO unless part of the delegation is explicitly directed elsewhere, for example, to a committee. The delegatee has the right to use any reasonable interpretation of the applicable board policies.

10. Monitoring: The board must monitor organizational performance against previously stated Ends policies and Executive Limitations policies. Monitoring is for the purpose of discovering if the organization achieved a reasonable interpretation of these board policies. The board must therefore judge the CEO's interpretation for its reasonableness, and the data demonstrating the accomplishment of the interpretation. The ongoing monitoring of board's Ends and Executive Limitations policies constitutes the CEO's performance evaluation.

All other practices, documents, and disciplines must be consistent with the above principles. For example, if an outside authority demands board actions inconsistent with Policy Governance, the board should use a 'required approvals agenda' or other device to be lawful without compromising governance.

Policy Governance is a precision system that promises excellence in governance only if used with precision. These governance principles form a seamless paradigm. As with a clock, removing one wheel may not spoil its looks but will seriously damage its ability to tell time. So in Policy Governance, all the above pieces must be in place for Policy Governance to be effective. When all brought into play, they allow for a governing board to realize owner accountability. When they are not used completely, true owner accountability is not available.

Policy Governance boards live these principles in everything they are, do, and say.

BIBLIOGRAPHY

Carver, John. *Boards that Make a Difference: A New Design for Leadership in Nonprofit and Public Organizations*. San Francisco, CA: Jossey-Bass, 1997.

Carver, John. *John Carver on Board Leadership: Selected Writings from the Creator of the World's Most Provocative and Systematic Governance Model*. San Francisco, CA: Jossey-Bass, A Wiley, 2002.

Carver, John, and Miriam Mayhew Carver. *Reinventing Your Board: A Step-by-Step Guide to Implementing Policy Governance*. San Francisco: Jossey-Bass, 1997.

Cousins, Don. *Leadershift*. Nashville, TN: Thomas Nelson, 2007.

Hull, Ted. *A Guide to Governing Charities*. Winnipeg, MB: Word Alive Press, 2011.

Oliver, Caroline. *Getting Started with Policy Governance: Bringing Purpose, Integrity, and Efficiency to Your Board*. San Francisco, CA: Jossey-Bass, 2009.

www.carvergovernance.com

ABOUT THE AUTHOR

Ted Hull is currently the President of Ted Hull Consulting and a Consultant with The Governance Coach™. He has a passion for coaching leaders and consulting with the boards of churches and charities, specifically in the effective implementation of Policy Governance®. He served on the staff of Grant Memorial Church in Winnipeg, Manitoba, Canada, where he developed and directed a counseling center. Subsequently he was the Director of Operations for Empower Ministries.

Ted lives in Winnipeg with his wife Lorna. He has two children and four grandchildren.

Ted Hull Consulting
204.898.6740
thull@TedHullConsulting.com
TedHullConsulting.com

What Does Board Coaching Look Like?

Teams in every sport need a coach. The coach usually doesn't play on the team. He or she understands the game and uses that understanding to develop a game plan that will help the team win. However no team wants its coach to put together a plan, walk into the dressing room, throw it down on the table and walk out. A good coach is constantly pressing the players toward excellence, while pointing out ways that the team can improve. That doesn't mean the coach is smarter or can play the game better. Rather, the coach draws upon his or her experience and understanding of the game and experience so that the players around them can succeed.

Boards are no different. They are teams. They need someone from the outside to provide a game plan for the team and the perspective that challenges the team to be the very best it can be.

The Governance Coach™ is that someone. The Governance Coach consultants have a seven step approach to coaching, designed on the basis of over 50 cumulative years of experience, called The REALBoard Excellence Advantage™. Here are the steps:

The Clarity Consultation™

This one day workshop provides an overview of the Policy Governance˙ system. It also provides time for questions and answers about how the system would work in your particular situation. By the end of the day your board will be clear whether it is ready to implement this governance system.

The Board Management Accountability Process™

Now that your board understands the principles of Policy Governance, your coach will facilitate the process of putting in place an initial set of policies which are unique to your organization.

The Alignment Process™

You have the basics of the Policy Governance model in place. As you begin applying the principles you notice that your board has certain structures and practices in place that need to be changed. Also you recognize that certain corporate documents, such as by-laws, need to be amended so that those documents align with your new governance structure. Now you need to take the steps to make those changes.

The Accountability Culture Enhancer™

Policy Governance seemed like a wonderful idea when you started. But without a culture of accountability, it is easy to postpone or even ignore the disciplines that are needed for it to work effectively. With The Accountability Culture Enhancer, your coach challenges your board to develop an ethos where accountability is the norm. Your board will be diligent in carefully assessing the monitoring reports it receives, rather than taking a cursory peek at the report or hoping that someone else looks at the report carefully. Your board will regularly evaluate its own meetings to make sure it focuses only on those items that are its responsibility rather than getting into the administrative weeds. Your board will have a plan for holding itself accountable for how it has agreed to conduct itself as it governs. Ownership linkage will be more than a good idea. Your board will have an initial plan by which it intentionally connects with its owners.

The Vision Refiner™

By now you have implemented an ownership linkage plan and know how to connect the information to Ends – the